Have Kids—Will Travel

Has changed the way families travel:

"You have highly inspired us! We homeschool and had planned to travel the world beginning when our daughter turned nine. This has given us the opportunity to bump that age up. We are already in the works of planning a trip to the east coast next year. We are using our flight credit card to pay our mortgage, groceries, etc. on. Of course, we immediately send the money to pay it off. Thanks so much for your inspiration and wonderful advice. You have literally made our dreams come true."

- THE MILLER FAMILY

"My son's assignment in school was to write about something he did that was fun over the summer. He told me that he didn't have anything to write because we didn't go anywhere. How pitiful we are. *Have Kids—Will Travel* will change our lives for the better. Thanks!"

- STEPHANIE ALLRED

"I just wanted to say that I ordered this book and it was awesome. It was so informative that we are going to use many of the "tricks" mentioned. It really is a great resource. Even my husband got excited about the opportunities"

- GENEVA B

"*Have Kids—Will Travel* is an answered prayer and dream come true. I found it to be a fascinating read, chockfull of little known travel secrets and tips. A million thanks to Dale and his family for sharing these fabulous and insightful travel secrets."

- DEBBIE ROSE

Have Kids—Will Travel

A Family Guide to Inexpensive Travel Anywhere in the World

Most of it FREE!

Have Kids—Will Travel

A Family Guide to Inexpensive Travel Anywhere in the World
Most of it FREE!

DALE & MICHELLE BARTLETT

BookWise
publishing

The world is a book
and those who do not travel
read only one page.

- St. Augustine

Have Kids–Will Travel
Copyright © 2009 by Dale and Michelle Bartlett
All rights reserved.

BookWise Publishing
65 E. Wadsworth Park Drive, Suite 110
Draper, Utah 84020
www.bookwise.com

Text & photographs by Dale Bartlett, Michelle Bartlett, and Brianne Bartlett
Editor: Toni Miller–RxEditing

To order this or any other publication call 435-245-3208 or visit
www.HaveKids–WillTravel.com

Cover design and book layout: Eden Design, Salt Lake City, Utah
web.mac.com/edendesign

ISBN: 978-1-60645-009-3
10 9 8 7 6 5 4 3
Third Printing

Dedicated to our wonderful family:

Our children, Brianne, Cameron, Devon and Marissa,
for letting us drag them all over the world.

Contents

foreword

Certainly, travel is more than the seeing of sights;
it is a change that goes on, deep and permanent,
in the ideas of living.

- MIRIAM BEARD -

I was visiting San Francisco with my wife when we decided to ride one of the city's world famous trolley cars. We took our place in an agonizingly long line that stretched halfway down the block. As we waited our turn a homeless man approached me and said, "Sir, for a dollar I'll tell you a secret to getting on the car without waiting."

Since I was intrigued about his secret and would have given him the money anyway, I handed him a dollar.

"Sir," he said, "have you noticed the trolley cars always leave the station half empty? It's so they can pick people up on the way up. See that corner?" He pointed to the nearby street corner. "That's the first stop."

"You're sure?"

"I wouldn't lie to you."

My wife and I walked to the corner wondering if we were fools but curious enough to take the risk. Sure enough, within two minutes a trolley car stopped at the corner and we stepped right on. A woman already sitting on the car just stared at us. "I waited more than an hour," she said.

Sometimes a little information can go a long way. And, in the case of *Have Kids—Will Travel*, it can even take further. Dale and Michelle Bartlett are travelers in the truest sense of the word. They've fully embraced the joy and enrichment of traveling and seen the world. They've had amazing experiences most people just dream about and done it on a shoestring. *And they've taken their children along for the adventure.* The effect of that on their family is far greater than the entertainment value.

If you have a desire to enrich your family's life through travel but feel it's not within your budget, this book should change your mind, if not your life. In *Have Kids—Will Travel,* the Bartletts teach not only the importance of family travel, but take you along with them through their adventures, sharing the tips and secrets that make travel fnancially possible for any family. Look for a lot of those "trolley tips"—simple and wise ideas you can trust. Dale and Michelle have personally used every technique they teach.

It is my hope that through the gathered wisdom of *Have Kids—Will Travel* you might experience the world more fully and develop memories that will live in the hearts of your family members forever.

—RICHARD PAUL EVANS

#1 *NEW YORK TIMES* BESTSELLING AUTHOR OF THE CHRISTMAS BOX

Preface

Many people have asked why we take our children on such elaborate vacations. We have many times thought the same thing. Michelle and I have repeatedly planned a second honeymoon or getaway to some exotic place that has consistently turned into a family vacation with the kids. Why?

Second honeymoons can wait, but our children's education and the time spent with them cannot. The opportunity we have had to provide an education where the world is the teacher has been one of the greatest benefits this kind of travel can provide. Not only do they experience new people and cultures, but they are immersed in the languages providing superior language skills. The time spent learning with your children will be the richest, most rewarding experience of your life. One of the greatest opportunities we have had has been to travel all over the world and see it through the eyes of our children.

We began this adventure nearly ten years ago and have learned various tricks to accomplish our travel at a minimal cost, sometimes even free. Our hope is to share our experiences with *you* so you can have the same enjoyment.

Many people believe this kind of travel is out of their reach. It's not. Planning and preparation are the keys. We hope you enjoy it as much as we have and will one day have your own tricks to share with others.

The intent of this book is not to be a travel guide with specific places to go, but rather a resource for inexpensive travel. The world is your destination and inexpensive travel is your key to exploring it.

—Dale Bartlett

Arrezo, Tuscany, Italy
(Sitting: Devon, Jennifer, Cameron. Standing: Dale, Michelle, Marissa, Brianne)

Introduction

According to the Travel Industry Association of America (TIA) the average traveler on his longest pleasure trip spends a little over a thousand dollars. In fact a thousand dollars provides only comparatively small trips of about seven nights and are no more than seven hundred miles roundtrip (TIA press release 5/18/04). This is an average. Taking into account that single people travel more than families (62%), the average family could easily double or even triple the cost for the same small trip.

To prove my point, consider a family of four on vacation to Disneyland for one week. If the cost of a hotel was $80 per night and food per day was $115, three days at Disneyland for four would cost around $600 (discounted); with souvenirs about $120, you're already at $1,695 and you haven't even left the house! As for transportation, whether or not you fly could be based on how much you have left in your vacation budget or how full the credit cards are. So flying or driving, you are easily over $2,000 and probably much more. But the kids will have fun, and everyone will see Mickey.

Now, what if I told you that for the same family of four *and* the same amount of money, maybe even less, you could spend two weeks (or longer) in Europe? Would you be interested?

Oh, yes . . . the kids might have to trade Mickey for the Eiffel Tower or swimming in a hotel pool for swimming in a crystal clear lake in the Swiss Alps. Or maybe you'll have to trade a long, hot car ride for an airplane ride with TVs and movies in front of every seat. Maybe you'll have to substitute a tour of the studio where they filmed *Jaws* for the beautiful city of Salzburg where they filmed *The Sound of Music*. Am I getting your attention? And to think all this for less than you were planning to spend anyway on a vacation less than seven hundred miles away from home.

Impossible you say? It can't be that easy? Well it *is* possible. Now I never said it would be easy. But it's not that difficult either. It just takes some planning and a little knowledge of how to travel almost free anywhere in the world. The whole point of *Have Kids–Will Travel* is to share with you some of the ideas and experiences our family has had as we have traveled the world for less money than it would cost to go to Disneyland. Not that I have anything against Disneyland. My point is this: do you want to explore a make-believe world or the real world?

Back in the winter of 1999 I noticed some very cheap fares to London. I asked my wife, "Wouldn't it be fun to have Christmas this year in London?" Her response was as I expected (and would be the response of any reasonable person), "We could never afford that." I dropped it for a time, but kept my eyes open for inexpensive fares as the year went on.

I also started noticing that we had done something that facilitates cheaper travel. A year earlier I had begun flying now and then for work and had joined an airline's frequent flyer's club. About the same time we had switched to an airline miles credit card. I noticed that the miles from the frequent flyer's club, the credit card, and the small amount of travel I was doing for work was really beginning to add up. So the first thing we did was change the way we purchased things, especially "big ticket" items. Instead of making purchases with check or cash, we would put them on the credit card and send the same amount to the credit card company, thereby always paying it off by the end of the month, but also gaining valuable airline miles.

This was the first lesson we learned in traveling cheap. By the time we were ready for our first trip, we had two free tickets to Europe. And that was just the beginning . . .

CHAPTER ONE

CHEAP FLIGHTS
Less Money, More Pixie Dust...

CHEAP FLIGHTS
Less Money, More Pixie Dust...

Our first international family flight was back in 2000. We spent three weeks divided between France and England with four children ranging in age from three to thirteen. We fully anticipated that this would be our "once in a lifetime" trip; little did we know it would actually be the first of many, each a little less expensive than the previous one. Though this first trip was relatively cheap (around $5500 for six of us over three weeks), we subsequently discovered that travel could and would cost much less. With this book, you have the added benefit of leveraging our many years of experience to make it possible for your family—whatever size or income—to travel the world as we now do, both inexpensively and *free*.

Over the years, we've become much more savvy—not only mastering several budget-stretching strategies, but also learning how to make the whole travel experience more meaningful and fun for family members of all ages. Despite any negative press regarding airline miles, frequent flyer plans can, *and do,* save a family hundreds, even thousands, of dollars. But if collecting miles just isn't your thing, there are numerous other ways to achieve substantial savings on both domestic and international flights.

FREQUENT FLYER PLANS

Many people believe that frequent flyers are people who, by necessity or choice, take numerous flights a year. Years ago that was probably true. Previously, miles were based only on actual miles flown. Today, however, nearly every purchase a family makes can add miles to an account. Now a "frequent flyer" may only fly once every couple of years, or not at all, but they can earn miles toward their next flight every single day.

Joining a frequent flyer/airline miles plan—and understanding how to accumulate miles even when you don't fly—is the easiest and fastest way to get free tickets. Most people don't realize just how quickly they can earn free flights—not just for themselves, but also for the whole family. However, it does require a little discipline.

Here's how our family saved over $11,000 on a single trip in just airfare.

The Frequent Flyer

Choose Wisely

There are several factors to consider when choosing a frequent flyer program. The significance of each factor varies from family to family.

One consideration is an airline's hub city. We chose Delta since the closest airport to our home is a Delta hub. This is convenient for us because we travel all over, but if most of your trips are to the same destination, it may make more sense to consider an airline with a hub in the vicinity of that destination area. Try to think ahead and select the airline that will be best suited to your long-term traveling needs. If you're planning trips to Europe, Asia or Mexico, it makes little sense to collect miles on Southwest Airlines or other carriers that fly only in the U.S. However, if you're planning trips to Florida, California or anywhere else in the U.S., a regional carrier like Southwest may be the best choice.

Check out an airline's flying partners—other airlines that you can either collect points with when flying or use when redeeming points. You may be collecting points on a domestic carrier that has limited choices for your future destination but is teamed up with several overseas carriers that provide a perfect fit. For example, Alaska Airlines partners with the SkyTeam Alliance, which includes Delta, Air France, Hawaiian Airlines, Qantas, and several more. So if you collect miles on Alaska Airlines, but want to fly to a destination not serviced by them, you still have many choices.

Choosing an airline with the most options available to the destinations you are seeking, either on its own or through one of its flying partners, provides you with flexibility. This comes in handy when you convert your miles to actual tickets. For example, we used our Delta miles to travel to Italy, but we flew to Washington, D.C. on Delta, to Paris and Florence on Air France, and on Continental Airlines for one leg of our return trip. Book all of your tickets through the airline with which you have the frequent flyer account but fly the carriers best suited to your destination. This gives you flexible destinations and provides you with more choices when using miles.

Make sure you have all the facts before making a decision. Specifically, read the small print in each airline's frequent flyer agreement to determine which one allows you the greatest flexibility in rolling miles over from year to year. This is essential because depending on the size of your family; it may take some rollover time to accumulate the miles you need for a free trip. Some airlines require one qualifying trip per year to carry miles over from that year to the next. Another airline only requires yearly activity, such as miles from a non-flying partner, on your account. Either way, you need to know the rules so you don't lose valuable miles.

The last factor to consider is how many ways a frequent flyer plan allows you to earn miles *without* flying. Most airlines have an associated dining program (check the airline Web site) as well as several non-flying partners that also award airline miles for spending money with them.

The most common non-flying partners are hotel chains and rental car agencies, but Netflix, cell phone companies, long distance carriers, Internet providers, restaurants, mortgage brokers, even florists are other possibilities. Best of all, these may be companies with whom you are already doing business.

Along with miles flown and non-flying partner miles, some airlines also offer extra miles for certain procedures and protocols such as buying tickets online, checking in online, signing up for a partner program or connecting through certain cities. United Airlines even awards miles for graduating from college. Check out the College Plus Program on the United Web site.

Consider an Airline Credit Card

For our family, the single largest contributor of miles is the credit card offered directly by the airline. As you compare frequent flyer plans, check out each airline's credit card plan to see which ones accumulate miles the fastest and/or have the least restrictions. Some plans offer double miles for certain dollars spent; some have no fees the first year; and some have fees that may be waived if requested. When you take full advantage of airline partners (flying and non-flying) and use your airline credit card judiciously (more on this later), the cumulative effect is far greater than what may be gained by just flying, even very frequent flying. Think of it as multiple mountain streams (of miles) all flowing into a huge reservoir (of future vacations).

To help you find the best program for your family, here is a list of airlines and their Web sites. Compare programs at www.webflyer.com/programs/ratings. In Canada, check out www.rewardscanada.ca.

Air Tran
A+ Rewards   888-327-5878   www.airtran.com

Alaska Airlines
Mileage Plan   800-654-5669   www.alaskaair.com

American Airlines
AAdvantage   800-882-8880   www.aa.com

ATA
Travel Awards   800-435-9282   www.ata.com

Continental
OnePass   713-952-1630   www.continental.com

Delta Airlines
SkyMiles   800-323-2323   www.delta.com

Frontier Airlines
Early Returns   866-839-2436   www.frontierairlines.com

JetBlue
TrueBlue   800-538-2583   www.jetblue.com

Midwest
Express Program   800-452-2022   www.midwestairlines.com

Northwest
WorldPerks   800-447-3757   www.nwa.com

Southwest
Rapid Rewards   800-445-5764   www.southwest.com

United
Mileage Plus   605-399-2400   www.united.com

US Airways
Dividend Miles   800-428-4322   www.usairways.com

Non-Airline Cards Offering Airline Miles

People often ask me about other credit card miles programs that are not associated with a particular airline. These work differently from airline credit cards and although they technically offer greater choices of carriers, they generally require either greater spending and/or a longer time to accumulate enough miles for free travel. With these cards, miles are accumulated only for purchases made with the card—usually one point per dollar spent. Some cards give two miles per dollar but increase the amount of miles needed for the reward, creating a net gain of zero. Once you have enough miles for a ticket, you purchase and pay for it just as you would for any flight with any airline. The credit card company then credits your account with the dollar amount equivalent to miles earned.

These credit card miles cannot be combined with other airline miles so you don't get the cumulative impact of combining airline miles with airline partner miles. Non-airline cards do offer more flexibility since you're able to use the miles with any airline. I prefer the cumulative effect provided by the airline card but only you can decide what is best for you and your family.

One site that keeps track of the current programs offering frequent flyer miles is www.freefrequentflyermiles.com. Several Web sites offer reward miles for shopping with an extensive list of merchants. These include:

www.clickrewards.com   www.travellerpoll.com
www.lendingtree.com   www.opinionplace.com
www.mypoints.com

Sign on the Dotted Line

Step 1 Choose a frequent flyer airline and sign up the entire family. Each family member needs a separate account as miles earned for actual flights can only be credited to the account of the ticket holder. Choose one account (usually the family member who flies the most) to accumulate all of the additional non-flying miles. Miles can be transferred later if necessary, but there is usually a fee associated with transferring miles.

Step 2 Sign up for that airline's credit card and watch the miles add up. Here is just one example of how quickly they can accumulate.

Do this . . .	and receive up to . . .
Sign up for and use credit card	15,000 miles
Add additional card holder	2,500 miles
Activate partner cell phone	7,000 miles
Activate partner Internet provider	7,000 miles
TOTAL	**31,000 miles**

Without even stepping into an airport, you have 31,000 miles—enough for one free round trip ticket in the United States and more than halfway to a free ticket to Europe! Most carriers require 25,000 miles for a domestic round trip and 50,000 for a round trip to Europe. Check the airline of choice to be sure. In the example above, miles continue to accumulate each month for the dollar amount spent on cell phones, Internet partners and credit card use.

Natalie, one of our newsletter subscribers, was so excited when she discovered that this procedure was even easier on Alaska Airlines.

"When I was flying on Alaska Airlines last weekend, they had a deal that when you signed up for their credit card, you received 20,000 miles—enough for a free round trip ticket. It did exclude Hawaii and Cabo San Lucas unless you had additional miles already, but they also offered a companion ticket for only $50—*and you can get another one every year.* The miles may be used and accumulated with several major airlines. When my family and I fly to Alaska to visit family, the cost is minimal."

The great thing is that it's really simple to both accumulate the miles and keep track of where they're coming from. When you book a flight you know you've got mileage miles coming, but when you book a flight with your airline credit card you may get up to three miles for each dollar spent *plus* the flight miles.

When booking any travel, be sure to tell the airline or travel agent that you are a frequent flyer and give them the appropriate account number. If you fly for business and don't make your own reservations, be sure the person booking the flight has your account information or that you provide it when you check in. Don't just assume that airline agents will automatically ask for this information. It's your responsibility to remember and provide it. It is possible to retrieve air miles after a flight, but the process is much more complex and time-consuming than simply providing the information beforehand.

A good site to compare the different credit card offers is: www.card-benefit.com/credit-cards/airline-mileage.htm.

Work the System

When you sign up for an airline credit card, don't get the gold or platinum version right away. Sign up for the basic card. Later if you want, you can earn more miles each time you upgrade to a new version. And when you do fly, remember to pay for cheap flights and use your earned miles to for the more expensive flights. A flight to Europe usually ranges between $1300 and $1600 and requires about 50,000 miles, a real cost of about four cents a point; a $175 to $250 flight to California requires 25,000 miles, which is about one dollar a point. Do the math— fly smarter, cheaper, farther and happier.

Every year you'll find new ways to amass miles. Sign up for email announcements of new miles offers, but follow through only if you're already considering using that partner. Don't let the lure of extra miles tempt you to overspend. Airlines also advertise special incentive offers throughout the year. Perhaps they'll provide additional miles when connecting through certain cities. Again, be prudent. Check to see if re-routing will add significant time and/or cost. If not, enjoy a new city, if only from the air, and smile as those extra miles add up.

If you're combining paid tickets with free tickets, it's important to determine which passenger gets which type of ticket. Often children's fares are lower than adult fares. And remember that free tickets do not accrue miles. If you have paid tickets, make sure that the person who is collecting the majority of the miles is one of the paid ticket holders so that they receive miles for that flight.

No matter how you accumulate miles, it's important to keep track. Remember that miles aren't always credited to your account right away. Miles earned while flying are usually credited directly after the flight. Partner miles, however, are not. These are usually credited once a month a few days after your statement date. Don't count on miles before they are credited. After each trip and when the point partners credit your account, confirm the miles that have been added. Make sure your records are the same as your frequent flyer account. The airlines allow very little time to correct any errors so make sure you contact them right away. Also be sure you have online access to your miles (usually through the airline's official Web site) and keep receipts and boarding passes for verification.

By following this plan, our family has accumulated three to six free airline tickets to Europe, or six to twelve within the United States, *per year.* Past trips have taken the six of us to France five times, England, Germany three times, Switzerland twice, Austria, Italy twice, Honduras, Belize, Mexico, Bermuda, the Bahamas, and all across the United States—all on the airline's dime! Well, almost all—even free tickets are subject to airport fees, taxes and fuel or baggage surcharges, but comparatively speaking, those costs were minimal.

Avoid Finance Charges and Debt

Do not accumulate debt with your miles credit card. Use it the same way you would spend cash or a write a check. Save up the money to pay for large ticket items such as a new couch or TV. Then instead of paying cash, use your airline miles credit card. After the purchase, pay the card provider online or mail a check for the same amount to the credit card company. Buy groceries, gas, and other errand items with the credit card. Then repay that amount when you get home. With online banking, it's easy—and free—to pay directly from your checking/debit account.

Use the card to pay monthly bills such as cell phone, utilities, Internet provider, doctors and any others that accept credit cards. See how quickly these regular purchases add up and, if you use the pay-as-you-go system, when the credit card bill arrives, you will have no finance charges, no balance due, and hundreds of free miles. For a big miles boost, contact your mortgage company to see if they accept payment by credit card. Be sure to ask if they charge a percentage for the use of a credit card and if they do, don't use your miles card.

Just remember to think of the card as a plastic check and pay it off as you go. If you rack up huge debt, you may accumulate a lot of miles but not be able to pay for anything else. The weight of that debt will take all the fun out of your travel. It takes discipline to manage a credit card that is used for virtually every purchase but if you can master the card, no pun intended, it will be worth it.

UNDERSTAND THE BOOKING PROCESS

People tell me that *using* their miles is the hardest part. It really isn't if you know a few secrets. It's always wise to read all the information on the airline's Web site but even these few basic facts should make the booking task a little easier.

1. Point Schedules

First, there are different point schedules with different rewards provided. For example, Delta has three levels of miles redemption. They simply call them low, medium and high. The higher schedule allows you to book any open seat. It is, of course, the most flexible but will cost you more miles. The middle tier requires fewer miles but has fewer seats available. If, like our family, you're only looking for flights at the lowest point level, you need to understand that many of these flights generally come with restrictions.

Expect blackout dates and be pleasantly surprised if your airline doesn't have them. Delta does not.

Avoid traveling during peak season. Typically the dates between March 20th and October 20th are peak times and dates between October 20th and March 20th are off-peak times, with Thanksgiving, Christmas and New Years typically at higher rates. This is not always the case, so check before assuming. Destinations in the southern hemisphere generally have opposite peak seasons and most tropical destinations are always peak. If they don't have any seats at the lower level, check to see if they have any first class or business class seats. Many times these use fewer miles than the higher level and who wouldn't want to go first class?

2. Timing

Don't assume that once you've accumulated enough miles you can just call the airline and book any flight, especially if you're buying other seats at regular or special fares (more on this later). Most airlines have a limited number of seats that they reserve for miles, so booking early is the key and *planning* is the key to booking early.

Many carriers also have limits on how early you can book. Be sure you know your airline's policy. If you're planning trips to popular destinations during peak times, you may have to book at the earliest available time. This could be as much as eleven months in advance. Booking off-peak travel is a bit easier, but earlier is still better.

Another key factor in securing free flights is flexibility. The more wiggle room you have regarding dates, airports, and routing, the greater your chances of hassle-free booking.

3. Booking

If you have enough miles to cover free flights for everyone, try booking online first. Most of the time you don't get very far, but if you're able to complete the transaction online, you save booking fees and, depending on the airline, may be rewarded with additional miles. Most of

the time we have to actually call the airline. Although this often means paying a booking fee, it also allows access to all of the airline's partners and the agent is able to check odd routes. Remember, you are responsible to ask if they have checked all partners and routing possibilities. You may have to route through multiple cities. A little inconvenience is often the trade-off for flying free. Be patient and polite. If you don't succeed in finding the right flights, thank the agent and try again later. You may reach someone who has a better command of the information or a flight may just have become available.

4. Buy or Borrow Miles

So you don't have enough miles for all the tickets you need? Sometimes you have to book a trip before you have all the miles needed for everyone going. Don't despair. There are a couple options depending on how many miles you need.

If you're just a few miles short at booking time, some airlines allow you to purchase additional miles. This can add up quickly, though, especially if the airline charges a processing or service fee as well. Some airlines may let you *borrow* miles for a month or two until you are credited from other partners such as credit cards.

5. Combine Miles Tickets and Purchased Tickets

Frequent flyer reward tickets may also be combined with regularly purchased tickets. Although this may not get everyone in the family to the destination free, it greatly reduces the overall cost. For example, imagine your family of four wants to go to London. You have enough miles for two free tickets and you've also found an airline promotion offering a $450 round trip fare to London. This means you're averaging $225 per ticket for each family member, a fifty percent discount.

First call the airline to book the two free tickets. Online booking isn't practical in this case. Be sure to have several departure and return dates in mind. You may need to go a day or two earlier or stay an extra day to find available flights. You may also need to fly into one airport and out of another.

Once you have found the free flights that best fit your schedule, have the airline hold this reservation without booking it for 24 hours—or more if needed. A number of airlines will hold them for thirty days. Then book the two paid tickets based on the itinerary of the free flights. Search sites that allow you to see the flight numbers and times of flights, or go directly to the airline or travel agent. Travel agents can be very helpful, but always check pricing to make sure you have the best deal. Once you have booked the matching flights, call back and book the free flights you had the airline hold. *Don't forget to do this.* If you call back after the hold expires, those flights may not be available. While all this does take some time and planning, your family of four is now off to London for less than what it might cost to fly to an adjoining state or province.

Here's one last thought on flexibility and combinations. If your final destination is in Europe or Asia, don't lose hope if tickets from your miles airline won't take you all the way. There are a number of very low cost airlines serving these regions and you can often book the last leg of your journey for as little as $24 one way. For example, if your final destination is Rome and your miles airline can only get you to Paris, you can fly very inexpensively from Paris to Rome on either EasyJet or Ryanair. For a list of lower priced airlines in Europe, go to www.low-cost-airline-guide.com. Pick your

TIP *When looking for cheap tickets using Web sites like Travelocity, it's best to check late at night. You'll save hundreds of dollars by staying up past midnight. Don't use Internet sites that prevent you from choosing specific flight numbers and/or times online. This could result in you and your kids ending up on different flights. Other good sites to visit are www.kayak.com and www.sidestep.com. Both of these provide listings of flight times and availability of the lowest fares on the net. Make sure you compare. Smart shopping pays off in the long run. An easy way to compare all of the search engines is to go to our Web site, www.havekids-willtravel.com and use our search engine which will bring all of the Web sites up for your comparison.*

departure and arrival cities and a list of available airlines will appear to the right. Once again, comparison shopping is the key to cheap travel.

Many airlines are trying to make it easier to use miles. For instance, Delta has a new *Pay With Miles* option that allows SkyMiles members with a Gold or Platinum American Express SkyMiles card to search for flights on www.delta.com and then pay for eligible tickets with miles, money, or a combination of both. Most airlines will also re-book your flight if the price comes down from the time you originally booked. This provides some security in booking early. Be careful, though; there may be re-booking fees and some airlines will only give you credit on future flights, not cash.

OTHER MONEY-SAVING STRATEGIES

Even without a frequent flyer plan, it's not too hard to find discounted fares. Again the key is always *flexibility*. The more flexible you are, the more likely you are to get a truly great deal.

Save Money with Internet Travel Sites

Many Internet sites offer discounted airfares. Tuesday night and Wednesday morning are often the best times to shop for bargains since many short-term deals are announced during this time period. Most sites use the same search engines and will come up with prices within a dollar or two of each other. Many sites also have separate pages of special offers. Some of these are last minute deals; others are the unsold remains from large blocks of tickets purchased by the consolidator. Either way, in order to take advantage of the bargains you must be willing to purchase—and sometimes travel—on the spur of the moment. Our site, www.havekids-willtravel.com, has not only combined all of the major search engines but also updates the latest deals every day. It's a great first place to start your search.

Other excellent Web sites include www.travelzoo.com and www.shermanstravel.com. These are very popular and offer some incredible deals. Log on and subscribe to their weekly emails. You'll be amazed at some of the offers.

Please note that sites such as these often require you to sign up to access their information. Usually the sign-up is free and the offers are actually fun to read. Browse the site frequently to get a better understanding of what deals are most suitable and doable for your family, but you must act quickly to get the deals. They are for very limited seats and, given the popularity of the site, they can be gone within hours of the email. We have seen cruise offers for less than ten dollars a night per person and flights as cheap as $49 *round trip*. No matter which sites you choose, always look for last minute special pricing categories.

Make Lemonade from the Airline's Lemons

1. Oversold Flights

Sometimes you have to be willing to be bumped to score a free ticket. Several airlines have cut back on the number of flights they offer. Because of this, many of the remaining flights are full or oversold. Whenever you can, book your travel so that you are on flights that sell out the most and be the first to volunteer to be bumped. Typically, if you're traveling to high traffic areas Sunday night, Monday morning, or Friday afternoon/early evening, the flight, more often than not, is likely to be oversold. I travel frequently to the same city and have found this to be true. The first thing I do when I get to the airport is ask if the flight is

TIP *If you use the well-known travel sites on the web to price tickets, make sure you clear your cookies after each search. If you're wondering what cookies have to do with airline fares, let me say first that I'm not talking about the chocolate chip variety. Rather, I'm talking about Internet cookies that are like fingerprints you leave as you visit a site. For example, suppose you find a low-price ticket but don't purchase it. Later you search again for the same fare on the same flight and it's not available. But that's not really because it's no longer available; it's just **not available to you** because the site knows you've already seen this fare and will no longer display it for you. Only higher priced fares are shown. Go to your Internet browser—Internet Explorer, Firefox, Safari etc.—to delete these cookies. Once you've done that, all available fares will again be available to you.*

full. If it is, I ask that my name be placed on the list of volunteers to be bumped. Sometimes my schedule doesn't allow this, but on most occasions I can pocket a quick three to four hundred dollars of airline "cash" for future travel.

Many airlines now offer vouchers to be used like cash with that airline. If you're offered a one-way or a round-trip ticket, make sure it's not limited by blackout dates that make it virtually unusable. If given a choice, take the airline cash voucher rather than a ticket. When you're bumped, ask if there is a quicker way to get you home on another airline. Remember, every carrier has a handful of partners. On one trip I was bumped twice. I received $750 in vouchers for a flight that only cost me $280. Even better, one of the re-bookings put me on a flight that was taking off five minutes *before* my original scheduled flight. Crazy, huh? I don't make up the rules; I just fly free because of them!

2. Overweight Flights

In addition to bumps for full flights, you can also be bumped for overweight flights. When fuel prices are high, airlines are especially careful not to exceed a certain weight. If baggage cannot be rerouted, agents will ask for volunteers to lighten the load. This is more common in winter than in summer. Again, when you check your bags, ask to be placed on the list of volunteers to be bumped. This way they can hold your luggage until they're certain you are actually on the plane. If there's no need to bump anyone, you and your luggage will be on the flight. If you are bumped, your bags should still be at the airport.

3. Involuntary Bumping

There are times when an airline involuntarily bumps all passengers, generally due to weather or mechanical difficulties. In these circumstances, airlines are not always under the same rules and obligations and you will not be offered a free flight. In this situation, patience is the key word. The person behind the counter has a lot of power and is often even more frustrated than you. Wait a bit. Let everyone else yell and complain. Then when things are somewhat under control, walk up and sympathize with the agent: "It must be very difficult having to deal with a situation like this. I was wondering, though, if there is any other way I might be able to get to my destination?" You will be amazed at how differently you'll be treated.

Agents have many options available and you want them to offer you the best. Often they can get you on another carrier's flight or reroute you a different way, creating a relatively minor delay. If that's not possible and you have to stay the night, ask for vouchers for food and lodging. A simple request may have you sleeping in a nice hotel while others are trying to turn plastic seats into beds at the airport. If you don't get anywhere with the person at the gate, go to the airline's information desk or back to the ticket counter and ask for a supervisor. The important thing is to always be polite and helpful. If you play the bump game properly, you nearly always win.

Frequently, any delay or cancellation of one flight increases the number of passengers on other flights that may already be nearly full. If you're involuntarily bumped due to any type of delay (and your schedule allows), ask if volunteers are needed on the next flight. If you're flying during a time when there are many delays and cancellations, your chances of being bumped are even higher.

If you fly enough, bumping can earn you credit for two or three free tickets a year. Remember, every airline's policy is different, so check the Web site before you fly. You should also know that these compensation rules do not apply to commuter airlines or charter flights.

TIP *Whenever you're bumped, always ask if it's possible to be placed in first class on the next available flight. If no flight is available until the next day, make sure you receive hotel and meal vouchers. Airlines will also pay for your transportation to and from the hotel but they rarely mention any of this unless you ask.*

4. Check Out Discount Airlines

If you're planning trips within the United States, discount airlines are your best bet. These so-called "no frills" carriers often have wonderful and easy rewards program. And if you are bumped, the dollar amount also goes much further. While it's true that major airlines often match and sometimes undercut discount fares, these smaller airlines do have their niche. Many have focused their routes on sunny locales such as Florida, the Caribbean, Aruba, California, and the American Southwest. They're hard to beat for cross-country travel.

I can personally attest to the value of the cross-country travel. Our family wanted to go to the East Coast for two weeks to see the historical sites of the Revolutionary War period and visit universities of interest to our older children. I had volunteered to be bumped twice on Southwest Airlines and had flown enough segments to accumulate three round-trip reward tickets.

I purchased two more tickets for my family with the bumped credit and bought the last ticket for $200 cash using Southwest's system-wide sale— $99 each way anywhere they fly. This meant that on average each of the six tickets actually cost less than $35. Southwest also has a Rapid Rewards program of its own where you can earn free flights by staying at hotels that participate in the Choice Privileges Plan. See www.choicehotels.com for details.

There are many other low-cost regional airlines. If you plan well in advance, you can get incredible deals. Be careful because they can come and go fast like Skybus, an ultra low price carrier. They looked great but only operated for a year before they threw in the towel. Other discount carriers that have been around for a while include Frontier Airlines, Virgin America, AirTran Airways, Spirit Airlines and Sun Country Airlines.

5. Consider Alternate Airports

One way that some of the discount airlines save money is by flying to airports a little further from major cities. You may be able to do the same thing with any airline or its partners. I have a friend in Seattle whose most frequent destinations are Charlton, Massachusetts and the D.C. Metro area. A few years ago she realized that flying into Providence, Rhode Island was not only cheaper but also much less stressful than flying into Boston. Flights into D.C. land at either National Airport (practically in the city) or Dulles (26 miles to the west). An excellent, and usually less expensive, alternative is Baltimore-Washington International, just 31 miles north of D.C. Just recently she needed a flight to Williamsburg, Virginia. Again it was cheaper to fly into Norfolk than to the capital city of Richmond. If you're looking online, be sure to access nearby airports when the option is presented or do your own research so you know what other airports to check for availability.

When you combine airfare with accommodations that are either free or highly discounted, it's easy to see how you can travel further and see more for much less. The key is flexibility and planning. Sometimes it takes both but either way, once you've experienced a vacation like our two weeks back East, you'll never fly the same again.

6. Spend a Little—Save a Lot

One last place to find incredible—even free—airfare is www.cheap-trips.org. This is a members-only site so you'll need to sign up and pay a fee. If you're thinking of doing a lot of travel, it may be worth it. Created ten years ago to overcome the problem of high airfare, this site specializes in deep discount rates from wholesalers, travel discounters, and air courier flights. There are dozens of ways to save on regular airfare and you can find very low airfares to virtually any destination worldwide. There are even ways to travel free.

TIP *If you have any questions about your rights as a commercial airline passenger, A Consumer's Guide to Air Travel is available from the Superintendent of Documents, U.S. Government Printing Office, Washington, D.C. 20402. The small fee is more than offset by the wealth of information.*

Again, the big key is flexibility. The more flexibility you have, the more opportunities for inexpensive travel.

7. Join a Charter Flight

Charter flights are private, usually organized by tour operators. The company that charters the flight pays the same price whether one person flies or a hundred, but the more people who fly, the cheaper the cost per person. A charter flight may be a good option if you're only looking for less expensive flights and you're happy with the whole package (car rental, hotel, etc.). Charters are inflexible and do not usually work well as cheap airfare when combining with miles. If you use charter flights, wait as long as possible to purchase tickets. Most airline prices increase as the flight gets closer to departure, but charters get cheaper as each person books. Make sure you keep a constant eye on pricing movement and availability, otherwise the flight may sell out.

8. Exploratory Travel—How to Hitch a Ride

This type of travel is for the highly flexible flyer. There are a few companies which will match you up with last minute cheap, unsold seats. You'll need to purchase a "contract" for the destination you plan on flying to within the next year. Then redeem your contract whenever the company matches you up with an airline that has an unsold seats.

How much cheaper are these seats? Like everything, it will vary depending on the time of year, etc. Always be a smart shopper and shop around, but the slogan on the Airtech site says, "If you beat these prices, start your own d**** airline!" Check them out at www.airtech.com and www.Airhitch.org.

9. Ride the Rails

If flying isn't for you, Amtrak Guest Rewards is a useful miles program that may also be combined with some airline miles programs. For example, miles are transferable to and from both Continental and Midwest

Airlines at a one-to-one ratio. Another advantage of Amtrak is that you can transfer miles to the Choice Privileges (Visa card) rewards program. Here's how it works: Currently 5,000 Amtrak miles (the smallest amount you can transfer) gets you 25,000 Choice Privileges miles. Each 5,000 Choice Privileges miles earns 1,000 miles with Air Canada, Alaska, American, Continental, Delta, Mexicana, Northwest, United Airlines, or US Airways. You may also redeem Choice Privileges miles for Southwest Airlines Rapid Rewards credits— 10,000 Amtrak miles yield 50,000 Choice Privileges miles which convert to 20 Southwest Rapid Rewards credits—more than enough for a free round trip ticket.

If you book an Amtrak trip within ninety days of signing up for the Guest Rewards program, you also earn 500 bonus miles. Amtrak programs do change frequently and often without notice, so it's wise to transfer miles as they accrue. Also be aware that Choice Privileges miles have a much shorter lifespan than miles from other programs. More Amtrak information is available at www.amtrakguestrewards.com. Details of the Choice Privileges Rewards program can be found at www.choicehotels.com.

To review . . .

To make the most of your airline miles program:

1. Choose one program (maybe two) and stick with it. Airlines reward loyalty and the miles will accrue faster.

2. Plan trips to popular destinations at times other than peak travel periods.

3. Book trips as far in advance as possible.

4. Have several dates in mind and ask for availability within a few days before and after your intended date.

5. If you don't get the dates you want the first time, wait a few days and call again. Circumstances change. Ask to be notified if your dates open up.

6. To realize additional savings, use Internet sites like Travel Zoo and Shermans Travel to find bargains. Remember to clear the cookies from your computer's browser after each site visit!

7. Take advantage of bumping whenever possible.

8. Fly into airports a little further from major cities.

Family Favorite

The airline credit card is our favorite way to rack up points in a hurry. We use it for everything we possibly can, pay it off purchase by purchase, and take advantage of every offer that makes sense for our family.

CRUISING

No Pirates in the Caribbean

## CHAPTER 2

CRUISING
No Pirates in the Caribbean

Flying is simply the means to an end. Cruising, on the other hand, is the experience. One of our favorite family vacations was a seven night Western Caribbean Cruise. Today's cruises offer an almost endless array of activities on shore as well as aboard ship. While some costs are inevitable, we have found many ways to cruise relatively inexpensively without giving up all the side trips.

FREE CRUISES

Sing for Your Supper

There's no question that cruising free is a much greater challenge than flying free. That said, it's not impossible either, but it does require some ingenuity and perseverance. Many cruise lines employ experts to entertain and/or inform their guests. If you have experience, knowledge, talent, or a skill that interests other passengers, the cruise line may provide you with free passage and meals in exchange for you sharing that expertise with others. Topics as diverse as "green" living, container gardening, and power shopping may be just what the cruise director is looking for. If your specialty is languages, a cruise offers a good opportunity to teach others simple phrases they can use at various destinations.

Securing free passage for your entire family will require either negotiating different opportunities for each member or creating a presentation the whole family can participate in with enough appeal to justify the number of cabins you need. The Osmond family could pull this off, but the rest of us may find it difficult. Still, even one free cabin greatly reduces your cost. If you or any family member has marketable knowledge or talent, contact the cruise line directly to negotiate terms. They may refer you to an agency that will make all the arrangements.

Become a Pseudo-Celebrity

Celebrities often cruise for free because they allow the use of their name to promote the cruise and agree to do an onboard meet-and-greet or book signing. On paper, free passage is compensation for the time they spend interacting with passengers. In reality, their mere presence guarantees enough bookings to more than cover their passage.

As a pseudo-celebrity, you probably won't be doing a meet-and-greet, but if you can pull together enough bookings, you can propose the same arrangement for free travel. The trick is getting enough people to go along with you. If you are in charge of a large event like a class reunion or multi-generational family reunion, gathering a hundred or so bookings may be quite doable. It will take a lot of work, but free sailing for your family makes the effort worthwhile.

MONEY-SAVING CRUISES

EasyCruise

If entertaining and recruiting sounds like too much work, or if a plethora of onboard amenities isn't your top priority, a stripped down "easy cruise" may be more to your liking. EasyCruise offers a new way to visit typical cruising destinations in the Caribbean, the Mediterranean, and the Greek Isles. More like floating hotels, these ships are much smaller than typical cruise liners and offer few to none of the onboard activities found on the big ships. They provide both transportation and lodging, but very little in the way of vacation experience.

EasyCruise is owned by the same company as EasyJet, one of the big discount European airlines. The ship docks around noon each day, allowing passengers to disembark and enjoy the sights and nightlife of that day's destination. It leaves each port before dawn the next morning. You don't even have to stay onboard for the entire cruise. Just hop on and off as you like and pay only for the nights you are onboard. The company currently offers a Caribbean itinerary with stops at six islands for less than $20 per night for an inner cabin. Mediterranean cruises start at about $60 per night with ports of call in Nice, Cannes, St. Tropez, Monaco, Genoa, Portofino and San Remo. Four additional itineraries are available in the Greek Isles.

Though certainly inexpensive, EasyCruise may not be the best option for all families. The company's target audience is twenty to forty year-olds (though one reviewer recalled seeing a "sea of white hair"). Parents with children under twelve are advised to "carefully read all information and then make an informed decision if this is the right type of holiday for them." Meals can be purchased onboard and daily maid service is also an added charge. These ships are for folks who want to maximize their time onshore. For more details, go to www.easycruise. com.

Ahoy Mate

If you want a real life sailing adventure, become a crew member on a sailing ship. The Russian training ship Kruzenshtern stops in Spain and Portugal, then sails transatlantic to Brazil, Uruguay, Argentina, Chile, Peru, Ecuador and Mexico. From there it heads across the Pacific to Hawaii, Eastern Russia, China, Australia, Madagascar, and South Africa, leaving Cape Town to return to Spain and Russia.

The ship charges 80 Euros (around $96) per day plus a membership fee of 55 Euros (about $66). Passengers sleep youth hostel style with twenty bunks to a room. Hands-on sailing won't work for younger children (for safety reasons there's generally a minimum age requirement anyway), but teenagers might enjoy the experience. If you're interested in this kind of adventure, a couple of sites are worth visiting. Go to www.tallship-friends.de. (This site is in German. Use a translation site to translate.) For a list of sail training opportunities, including the Kruzenshtern, go to www.tallshipbounty.org for information on HMS Bounty.

Luxury on a Budget

If you want a regular cruise at a great price, a travel consolidator may be your best bet. These companies buy up popular and last-minute cruise space and offer it at significant savings. There are many consolidators to choose from including www.bestpricecruises.com, www.cruisecompany.net and www.cruiseforless.com. Start with these or type "cruise

consolidators" into your search engine and find your own favorites.

If your schedule doesn't allow last minute cruising, the best time to get the best price is during what is called the "wave" season which runs from January through the middle of March. This is when the majority of cruises are booked and cruise lines offer lots of incentives and promotions (upgrades, Kids Sail Free programs, shipboard credits, etc.) in order to fill staterooms early. Cruising has become increasingly popular over the last few years, which has also resulted in many new ships. Twelve cruise vessels were launched in 2007. With more spaces to fill and the economy forcing some folks to cut back, there may be even better deals in the coming years.

Even with a full service cruise you should keep your eye out for great deals. Sites such as HaveKids-WillTravel, ShermansTravel and Travel-Zoo (all discussed in Chapter 1) are great sources for bargain cruises. We found an incredible eight day, seven night Western Caribbean cruise to Honduras, Belize, Cozumel, and a private island owned by the cruise line. We booked the kids into an inside cabin and ourselves into a balcony cabin for an average cost of $433 per person. Using airline miles to get to Miami and hotel reward miles for our nights in Miami, we enjoyed an incredible, and incredibly inexpensive, vacation.

Repo Cruises

As seasons change, so do cruise destinations, especially in the spring and fall. This is when cruise lines move their ships from one home port to another and they don't want to move them empty. This repositioning of ships has created some one-of-a-kind cruise experiences at greatly reduced prices. Repo cruises tend to be longer and have fewer, but sometimes more interesting, ports of call. To entice passengers during this typically non-cruise period, cruise lines may offer special incentives such as cooking classes, wine tasting, or free airfare (remember, these are one-way cruises), as well as reduced booking rates. There is plenty of information on repo cruising online. One helpful site is www.expert-cruiser.com/advice/repo. Not all of these cruises will be kid-friendly, so check them out carefully.

SHORE EXCURSIONS

Twenty years ago cruising was all about shipboard amenities. Today, even though those amenities have increased and improved, most cruises offer a wide variety of activities onshore. If booked through the cruise line, these activities range from roughly $45 to $300 per person. Had we booked through the cruise line, most of the excursions we chose would have been in the $59 to $79 range, adding over $1200 to the cost of our trip. Not wanting to put out that much extra money (even on an airline credit card), we quickly learned how to save hundreds of dollars on these activities. Here's how we cut costs on that Western Caribbean cruise mentioned earlier.

Port of Call—Roatan, Honduras

Not every day in the tropics is sunny. We found that out the drizzly morning we arrived on the island of Roatan. We were welcomed by the local tour mobs, among which we negotiated an eight-passenger van with a driver and a guide. These were ours for the entire day. We took a full tour of the island, stopping off at interesting shops, an iguana park, and a wonderfully secluded beach where we did some snorkeling. Onboard the ship a similar trip on a tour bus would have cost $59 for each person. Our private tour cost exactly half that, including the snorkeling. We got to go where we wanted, when we wanted, and with guides who became our friends by the end of the day. The tour bus only stopped at predetermined locations and the snorkeling excursions booked from the cruise line were all cancelled because of rough water and the storm. Our guide had taken us to a different, storm-protected side of the island. Not only did we spend half as much, we also had twice as much fun.

Port of Call—Belize City, Belize

This day we split up with my parents going on an ATV excursion and the rest of us heading off to explore the Mayan ruins of Altun Ha. Once again we negotiated onshore for the best deal, ending up with a driver who gave us a tour of the city, a personal tour of the ruins and a tour through the rainforest— all for around $25 a person instead of the $54 for a pre-booked impersonal tour without the rainforest. On the way back to the ship, we even asked our guide to stop at a house where a man put on a show about snakes. The kids got to handle the snakes, including a hefty boa. The ruins were incredible and were made even more special with the personal history given by our driver.

Port of Call - Cozumel, Mexico

When in Cozumel, forget everything you think you know about traveling in Mexico. The island is clean, safe, and very tourist friendly, without the constant hounding to buy this or that. By now, additional families on the cruise had discovered that we did things a bit differently and much more cheaply. Several asked if they could join us and by Cozumel we had quite a group that increased our buying power. We really wanted to go to the Mayan ruins of Tulum that are on the mainland and reputed to

TIP *There are times when booking through the ship does make sense. While our family explored the ruins and played with snakes, my parents took an ATV ride through the jungle. Knowing only a few ATVs were available, they chose to book ahead through the cruise line. In this case the extra cost was well worth it because the experience would have been missed if they had waited.*

be incredible. After talking with several drivers and tour operators, we realized that driving to and from the ruins would use up all but half an hour of our onshore time. The trip was technically possible, but not at all practical. Instead, we chose an excursion that was probably more educational and definitely more relaxing. The driver and guide for our group was a historian. He took us to some ruins on the island, gave us

TIP *Another time when it's better to book an excursion with the cruise ship is when there's a chance of not getting back to the ship on time. If you book through the cruise and the tour returns late, the ship will still be waiting. If you return late on your own, you incur the cost and inconvenience of meeting the ship at the next port.*

a tour of the island, and shared some incredible history lessons as well. He also took us to a private beach and provided snorkeling gear for anyone who didn't already have it.

We enjoyed some of the best snorkeling we have ever experienced. Fish by the hundreds surrounded us, dove with us, and followed us. The beach also had a restaurant with wonderful food at reasonable prices. When we left the beach, our driver took us into town for some shopping. It wasn't the trip we had planned, but it turned out to be more incredible than we could have imagined.

Always do your research online before a cruise. Discover what activities and resources are available at each port of call. Look for Web sites that include comments and suggestions from previous cruise passengers. Compare this with information on the tours recommended by the cruise lines. Be open to alternate plans and ready to negotiate when you get off the ship. And remember that sometimes it's smarter to book ahead.

To review . . .

- It's hard to cruise for free, but discounts are available. Remember the Internet is your friend.
- If you can't set sail on a moment's notice, book during the Wave season for best prices.
- Sometimes (but not always) it's better to arrange shore excursions on your own.

Family Favorite

Our favorite cruise line is Norwegian. We love their freestyle cruising, which lends itself well to family travel. Kids can't always wait until a pre-appointed time to eat and not having to deal with hungry children is a big help to parents. Norwegian also provides wonderful programs designed specifically for children, "tweens," and teenagers. These onboard activities allow kids to meet other kids their age and enjoy some time away from the grown-ups while still under discreet supervision.

LODGING

Never Sleepless in Sicily

## CHAPTER 3

LODGING
Never Sleepless in Sicily

We travel to new places so we can explore, not sit in a hotel room. We only saw the inside of hotels late at night and were out exploring again early the next morning. We didn't seek out the most glamorous of hotel rooms; we only asked that they were clean and comfortable. Many nights our children slept head to toe, two to a single bed, with the youngest in bed with us. On other trips we packed a blow-

up mattress and a pump, which worked very well and provided a bit more room. Because our free nights were with Marriott, those rooms were much bigger. Our free nights have often been some of our best accommodations.

Having stayed in over a hundred different places in a dozen countries, we've learned two important things. First, there are many options beyond hotels. Second, how much you spend on lodging may depend simply on how adventurous your family wants to be.

NOTE: Nearly all the information in this chapter relates to hotels and other lodging in Europe. Most of the principles will apply anywhere, but it's always wise to consult region or country-specific Web sites or books regarding travel in other areas.

HOTELS

For many, the comfort and ease of a hotel is the only option. Understand that most hotels outside of the United States are not like hotels in America. They are much smaller and in many locations in Europe they have a different rating system. It's important to know that the Europeans rate their hotels by stars, one to five. The number of stars is directly related to the amenities offered, but the system does not correlate with the cleanliness or condition of the rooms. A one or two-star hotel can be much more enjoyable and less expensive than a rundown three-star with a restaurant and private bath.

In Europe, most rooms have either one double or two single beds. It's very difficult to find rooms with two double beds. Ask! I can't stress this enough. The hotels want your business and can usually accommodate you if you ask. We have frequently had additional beds (roll-a-ways and even cots) brought into a room. Also be aware that smaller, private hotels may deal only in cash or traveler's checks.

If your sights are set on a hotel experience, here are a few tips to make your stay a bit less expensive.

Earn Free Nights with Points

At one time our family spent over three weeks in Europe and only paid for three nights' lodging. We used Marriott reward points and redeemed them for some of the nicest hotels we've ever stayed in.

Like the airlines, hotel chains offer reward points. Because you need fewer points for a night's stay, it's sometimes easier to receive free nights than free flights. Again the key is planning and loyalty to a chain is important. It's also important to consider your family's most frequent destinations before deciding which chain to pledge that loyalty to. If you're traveling within the U.S. your choice may be different than if you go abroad. Hotel chains also have partners, just like the airlines, and offer credit card point redemption. Most chains also reward loyalty. Some show their appreciation for points clients by upgrading their rooms. Rewards of upgrades also come as you accumulate status by staying frequently with one chain.

Most hotel points are based on the dollar amount spent at that hotel. The more you spend with them, the more points you get. Others reward you with so many points per night, no matter what you spend, or a free night after so many stays. See which program will work best for you and make a decision based on the type of traveling you currently do. I recommend concentrating your efforts on one points program at a time.

Sign up for the hotel's associated credit card, just as you did with your airline. When you have all the points needed for your flight(s), put that card away and switch your focus to the hotel points card.

As with airline rewards, hotel bookings should be made well in advance and it's important to do some research before booking. Even within the same chain, hotels in Europe may be different from their counterparts in the U.S. For example, always check the location and specific room accommodations of a hotel before making a reservation. These factors can cause "free" to become quite costly. In Rome, for example, we wanted to book a room at the Marriott Courtyard. The hotel was wonderful but none of the rooms could accommodate more than three people. This meant we would need two rooms, which required either more points or a shorter stay. If you leave these decisions to the last minute, you may have to spend more. On this same Rome vacation, the hotel was located near the airport, which is about 25 kilometers from the city. The hotel offered a shuttle, but we neglected to check the cost before we arrived. With seven of us, the round trip price to Rome would have been over $150 per day. Since a rental car was only around $60 per day, we extended our time and drove ourselves.

Seek Out Cheap Hotels

Your local travel agent is probably not the best resource for finding a good, clean, inexpensive foreign hotel. Inexpensive generally implies the hotel's budget doesn't include promotion agents which means you have to find these bargains yourself. Decide what part of town you wish to stay in. Try to avoid the main thoroughfares. Parking in these areas is often a hassle and the noise can keep you awake at night. Look for hotels back a few streets.

A good source of information is the *Let's Go* guidebook series. Available at local bookstores and online for about $16, *Let's Go* books are produced by the Harvard Student Agencies and are an excellent source of information on lower cost hotels. The books provide concise descriptions of rooms and amenities. These listings are verified annually by traveling students. It's best to get a guidebook for each country you're visiting rather than regional books like *Let's Go Europe*, because city-specific information is quite limited in the regional books. The savings you realize using this series more than compensates for the cost of multiple books.

TIP *Europe has its own discount hotel chains, many of which cater to family stays better than the brand name hotels you find in the United States.*

Another great place to look for cheap hotel deals is www.flyertalk.com. Go to the forum section; click on Miles & Points and then on Hotel Deals. Check the site often as new deals show up all the time. There is also a Web site from the Netherlands (www.dakloss.nl) that has wonderful hotel deals and three percent of the proceeds go to help the homeless in Amsterdam. It's worth a look. You get great rates and benefit humanity at the same time. A third option is to run an Internet search for the tourist office in the city you plan on visiting. These offices have a complete listing of the hotels available and are very helpful. *Let's Go* guidebooks also list the tourist offices throughout the area covered.

Avoid City Centre

Downtown real estate is notoriously pricey. So are big city hotels. Look for lodging just outside larger towns or tourist hotspots. The cost of public transportation into town will likely be much less than the cost of in-town parking and you'll avoid the hassle of city traffic. Venice, for example, is a beautiful city with quaint hotels but it's very difficult to get around and very expensive, especially during the

high tourist season. If you stay in the city, you must park in a parking garage and take your luggage with you on a water bus. When you reach the neighborhood of your hotel, you still have to haul the luggage from the water bus stop to the hotel itself. There are no taxis or cars in Venice. There was also not a single hotel with a room that accommodated more than three people. At the low end we would have spent over $300 to sleep each night.

However, just outside of Venice in the city of Mestre, there were many options. We chose the Novotel, which had a family suite for $120 per night. We still needed to use our inflatable mattress, but all seven of us fit in one room. At times the kids will bring a friend along. In this case it was Brianne's friend Jenny. From the hotel we walked a block to a public bus, which took us directly into Venice for one euro apiece. The buses were more like motor coaches, and the bus drivers were very helpful and friendly. You do need to purchase your bus ticket beforehand at a newsstand or ask at the hotel.

TIP *There is one little-known secret that can get you an inexpensive hotel room in the very heart of Paris. The Hotel Dieu Hospitel (yes, it's the sixth floor of a hospital) may sound like an unlikely place to stay, but it's clean and right next door to the Notre-Dame Cathedral. Go to www.hotel-hospitel. com/ang/accueil.htm for more information or to book a room. Not many people know about this little secret so you may get some strange looks when you ask where the hotel is. But you can't beat the rate. It's around $80 per night for a single and $95 for a double and the location is one of the best in Paris.*

TRAVEL HOUSES, GUEST HOUSES, BED & BREAKFASTS

Hotels are fine but can be very impersonal—and cramped— but they're less busy over the weekend and often offer incentives for those days. I recommend staying in hotels on the weekends and Bed & Breakfasts during the week.

Bed and Breakfast establishments are owner-run and often more accommodating to families. They may have family suites or large rooms available. Call and talk directly to the owner. Tell them your family's size and needs, and then negotiate the best rooms and rates. Weekends are the busiest times for B&Bs. You'll have a better chance getting a great rate on a weekday.

On our first trip to Europe we traveled through France and then England. I'm uncertain whether it was because we could finally fully understand what was being said or because our hosts were simply charming, but our first night in the port town of Dover, England, was pure delight. We stayed in the West Bank Guest House of Mr. and Mrs. Michael (www.westbankguesthouse.co.uk). What a treat! The Michaels were absolutely wonderful hosts. For a little less than $13 per person (the family room rate at the time), we were treated like royals, including a wonderful breakfast of "bangers" (English sausage) with ham, eggs and toast, flavors we can still taste to this day. Our children were enthralled with both the local accent and the warm welcome the Michaels gave our family.

RESERVATIONS

Is it important to have reservations? Yes and no. It may depend more on the time of your travel. If it is during peak times (July and August for Europeans), reservations are always a good idea. If you're traveling off-peak, you can get a good room most places without a reservation. Many of the smaller, cheaper hotels don't even take reservations. If you happen to visit a city or town during a festival, you should have reservations. This is another reason to do proper research ahead of time. Also check online with local tourist offices. Ask for information on local festivals and whether they recommend reservations during the time you have planned your trip. If you do find yourself without accommodations during a festival, first drive around a bit, watching for signs advertising Bed & Breakfasts or other private lodging. You may be surprised to find wonderful accommodations in a most unlikely spot. Remember the Hotel Dieu Hospitel in Paris? If that doesn't work, try towns and villages on the outskirts of the festival city.

When you're "cold calling," ask first for the type of room you need and then ask to see the room. Don't be shy and don't hesitate to politely decline if you don't like the accommodations. Always negotiate the price. One night in France when we purposely had no plans or reservations, we began to look for signs for the *chambres d'hôtes* and eventually found an out-of-the-way gem just between Cernay-les-Reims and Reims. The La Bertonnerie, charmingly converted from an old garage or stable, included a two-story family chamber with breakfast brought to our room. Our stay was delightful.

Stay in Smaller Towns and Villages

We learned about staying in smaller towns and villages when we had car trouble in the small French town of Pré-en-pail. Many of these villages have wonderful family-owned hotels. In Pre'-en-pail, the family also ran the restaurant. Along with our host's duties as hotel and restaurant owner, she also served our table and would scold our children (in French) into eating all their food, especially the vegetables. The rooms were huge and very reasonably priced. They also provided our first experience with a bidet, which fascinated our four-year-old. Rather than seven of us being cramped in one small room in a hotel, here we could spread out. For less money we had two rooms and everyone had their own bed. While it's true that the language barrier increases beyond the larger cities, we had a wonderful time.

In France, look for signs for *chambres d'hôtels*. In Germany, look for homes with a *Travel Haus* sign. In England you may even find some inexpensive castle lodging. All of these are really more or less Bed and Breakfasts but they charge per person and the rate can be reasonable if negotiated. Ask for discounts for small children and infants. Many times, if asked, owners will waive the charge for younger children. Do compare the per person charges to room rates. If your family is large, the per-person charge may not be the best deal after all.

HOME EXCHANGES

Many cost-conscious families just like yours are willing to exchange homes. This concept goes back hundreds of years to when members of Europe's royalty simply contacted the king or a duke in the next country and asked permission to use his castle while on vacation. Now it's as easy as going online. Exchanges involve minimal risk. Most exchangers are stable, upper-middle class folks who love traveling. While an occasional glitch is inevitable, most participants have nothing but praise for the program.

How it works

List your home with photos and a description of where you live and the things to do in your area. Other members searching for places to visit contact you about an exchange. At the same time, you contact association members living where you would like to stay. Eventually, an appropriate match is achieved where you stay in their home and they stay in yours—sometimes during the same time period, sometimes not.

You can even exchange cars, thereby eliminating another big vacation expense. Before you do an exchange however, check your homeowners insurance. Most policies treat exchanges just like any other visitors in your home, but read the fine print or call your agent. Also check your car insurance if you choose to exchange vehicles and see if you will need any additional coverage during the time of exchange.

The home exchange program can work two different ways. First, decide where you're going and send out inquiries in that area for others looking to exchange. If you don't find an exchange partner however, you will need a back up plan such as hotels or rentals. Or you can be open to any possibility, wait until inquiries start coming to you, and be assured of an exchange. If you wait for offers,

TIP *If the home exchange program offers a printed directory, you will want to purchase it for at least the first year. This gives you easy access to all the current members with descriptions of their homes and contact information. Even if you don't renew, you may be able to use the book for future exchanges.*

you need to be somewhat flexible in order to work with the exchange family's schedule. Once you have a likely exchange, start corresponding with that family. Negotiate the time your home is available. Some people are exchanging vacation homes rather than private residences and, as a result, are more flexible and may allow you to use their properties with the guarantee of a future stay at yours. Negotiate all the details: terms, time of year, length of stay, number of people allowed, etc.

Surf the Web

We belong to several home exchange programs and have become an affiliate of www.JewettStreet.com, one of the fastest-growing and easiest sites to use. Once you join, access the advanced search section and check the affiliation of Have Kids–Will Travel. Then search for other *Have Kids–Will Travel* families. If you can't find an exchange that way, broaden your search until you find a home that suits your needs.

TIP *Don't think your house has no appeal. We live in a small town and when my wife approached me with this idea, I told her no one would want to come here. But they did. We have had offers for homes in Belgium, France, Germany, South Africa, and England. The offer in South Africa was incredible. The property was part of a private game preserve, edging against the ocean where you could sit atop cliffs and watch the whales swim by. Unfortunately, we had to pass this one up due to timing conflicts.*

Other home exchange programs we have enjoyed are the International Home Exchange Network at www.ihen.com and Homelink International at www.homelink.org. Homelink International also has a U.S. site at www.swapnow.com. Homelink International is more expensive—between $75 and $145 per year, depending on the options you choose—but it has more members and that means more options for you. And honestly, even at $145, it's well worth the cost. Considering the average exchange is two weeks, that's less than $12 per night.

An inexpensive program is Green Theme International (GTI) at www.gti-home-exchange.com.

Don't give up

Many home exchange members list homes that are also available for rent if an exchange is not possible. We had our hearts set on visiting Italy, but couldn't find a home exchange. However, one of the families we contacted had a restored farmhouse in Tuscany that they were willing to rent to us. The cost of this four-bedroom, two-bath home was $57 per night. It slept eight and had two bathrooms, which came in handy with four girls getting ready each morning.

The Vineyards of Capezzana

This wonderful home was part of the Bonacossi Villa, owned by the Count and Countess Bonacossi and originally built for one of the daughters of the Medici family of Florence. Our hosts met us in Florence, treated us to a fantastic Tuscan meal, introduced us to their family and then drove us out to the farmhouse. They also arranged a tour of the Villa itself, as well as a tour of the wine and olive oil facilities.

600 year-old farm home in Capezzana, just outside of Florence Italy

In this "base camp" we were able to relax, surrounded by vineyards and groves of olive trees dating back more than 2000 years. Across the valley, an ancient wall surrounded a little hill town. We could see the lights of the town from our bedroom window at night. A two-hour hike over the next mountain took us to Vinci, the birth place of Leonardo da Vinci. No cramped hotel room could possibly offer so much.

Tenuta Di Capezzana   *Marcello and Alessandra Contini Bonacoss*

RECIPROCAL HOSPITALITY

There are a couple of ways to receive free lodging by reciprocity. First, some of the home exchange sites also offer hospitality exchanges. You negotiate a stay with a host family during your vacation and in exchange they stay with your family on a future vacation.

The second method is to host foreign exchange students. We highly recommend this for any family, especially if you have children in the same age bracket as the exchange students. Hosting an exchange student is a wonderful way to get to know other cultures and learn about other counties you may want to visit. Often you will be invited to visit the student's family, sometimes even invited to stay in their homes. While this is not the main reason we host exchange students, it has certainly been a pleasant advantage. We now have close relationships with families in many different countries and have enjoyed wonderful times visiting them.

No matter how we find a hospitality exchange, it has become our favorite way to stay in any country. Have Kids—Will Travel is developing our own hospitality exchange at www.familyhospitalitynetwork.com. If you are only interested in England, try www.staydontpay.net. Most hospitality sites are designed for single travelers only, but others accept families, so do your research.

We find the more we travel, the more friends we make and the more opportunities avail themselves. While on a trip to Jackson Hole, Wyoming, we met a charming woman from Wales in the hotel laundry room. She was enthralled with our children. As we talked about our various travels, she invited us to stay with her in Wales if we ever had the chance. We have not yet had the opportunity, but that type of experience happens more often than you might think. On another occasion in England, we met a couple about our age with children close to our own in age. As we talked, they invited us to dinner at their home and offered use of their washer and dryer so we could catch up on our laundry. We still keep in touch with the family and have wonderful memories that will last a lifetime. Don't be shy. You never know where your next adventure will take you.

LESS CONVENTIONAL LODGING

Friends of Nature

We came across this wonderful way to stay very inexpensively while visiting friends in Switzerland. These friends are members of Natur-freunde (Friends of Nature), a group committed to providing environmentally sound leisure-time and travel programs. The organization runs over a thousand Friends of Nature Houses in Europe and elsewhere around the globe, including California and

TIP *When traveling in the spring or fall, be prepared for significant drops in temperature at night.* Nepal. The accommodations are very basic. Some had showers, some didn't, but all had indoor plumbing and toilets and were very clean. These Alpine hostels are available to the public but are much cheaper for Naturfreunde members. Because our friends were members, we were able to stay for around $10 a night. The jingle of cowbells outside our room helped us overlook the sparse bathroom facilities. Naturfreunde chalets have many rooms with multiple beds and are very accommodating to families. There are similar accommodations in other European countries.

Our chalet had a nice restaurant that was a bit pricey, but not bad when averaged with the $10 room. We brought our own food and prepared it in the house kitchen. A stroll down the dirt road led us to a wonderful dairy farm where we were able to purchase milk, cheese and other items. The view of the Alps was breathtaking and a variety of day hikes led to incredible rivers, mountaintops, glaciers, and waterfalls. We weren't able to resist the urge to take pictures. We made a 360 degree turn to capture all of the landscape, and when we had come full circle, we started all over again because the light had changed and given the mountains a whole new look.

The countryside is filled with glacier-fed lakes with the clearest water you will ever see. Swimming in them is wonderful. In the town of Thun, about 20 miles from the capital city of Bern, you can jump off bridges and float downstream—a great way to refresh yourself after a day of exploring.

To learn more about Naturfreunde, visit their Web sites. The Swiss site is www. naturfreund.ch. There are also sites for Germany, France and others. Run an Internet search for Naturfreunde and keep in mind that most sites are not in English. You may need to cut and paste information into a translation site such as www.babelfish.altavista.com or www.freetranslation.com. Other translation sites are also available. Some are better than others. You can also pay for "human" translation.

Camping

Our family has never camped outside of the United States, but this is a fantastic way to save on the lodging portion of your trip. Europe has some wonderful campgrounds and many can provide you with tents and other necessary equipment. Let Google identify numerous Web sites to help you find the right campsite for your family, or go to www. alanrogers.com and check out the Alan Rogers guide books which are designed for camping throughout Europe.

Europe's campsites are often rated by stars like hotels. One-star campsites are fairly basic and becoming increasingly rare these days as owners strive to improve amenities, gain extra stars and attract more customers. Two-star campsites are by far the most numerous and generally provide a reasonable level of comfort. Municipal (city or state-owned) sites, often found on the edge of towns and villages, usually fall into this category, though a few aim for higher ratings. Three and four-star campsites nearly always provide quite a high degree of luxury, often including first-class restaurants, extensive entertainment programs, and beautifully landscaped swimming pools and sports facilities. It is more like staying in an open air luxury hotel than the Boy Scout experience most Americans associate with camping.

To review . . .

- Use hotel points earned either through stays or credit card.
- Accept (and give) hospitality through a home exchange program or informally with people you meet.
- Check on rental options when an exchange isn't possible.
- Stretch your budget with a combination of points, hospitality, hotels, B&Bs, and hostels.
- Remember that one or two-star hotels are less expensive and often more appealing.
- Bed and breakfast inns, including Travel Haus and chambers d'hôtes, offer larger rooms at reasonable prices.
- Let's Go hotel guidebooks are well worth the investment.
- Use Friends of Nature or other family-oriented hostels.
- Be adventurous. Go camping. Try Alan Rogers' camping guidebooks.

Family Favorite

This is where it's difficult to pick just one—between the castle we stayed at in France (which was free) or the farmhouse in Italy (around $50 per night). The secret is to keep searching.

VACATION EATS
Pizza, Pastry and Ratatouille

CHAPTER 4

VACATION EATS
Pizza, Pastry, and Ratatouille

Eating in a different country is always an adventure. One day in Germany my taste buds were primed for a döner pizza. Döner is a seasoned meat mixture, often beef and lamb, much like a gyro. In Germany, döner is pronounced doona (or so I thought). The first mouthful of my eagerly anticipated meal made it very clear that the "meat" was neither beef *nor* lamb, but tuna—*not* my favorite pizza topping! Make every effort to pronounce words clearly.

Eating out anywhere can strain a budget and folks often underestimate, or even ignore, the potential for overspending in this area. In the U.S., numerous family-friendly restaurants and buffets cater to cost-conscious travelers. We have four children and our vacations usually include lots of walking, which naturally works up a good appetite. Children are happier when they are well fed. Just like adults. So what's best to eat and where do you get it?

Managing a food budget can be tricky if you are overseas and not sure how much the next meal may cost. Restaurants are expensive and often you leave only half filled. Cafes are better, but in the touristy areas they can also be very expensive. The information that follows explains some of the more important cultural differences relevant to eating in Europe as well as a number of cost-cutting alternatives to full-service dining.

Appreciate the Diversity of Cultures

Even though the English language is prevalent in most countries, Europe is not the United States. Nowhere is that more clear than in food choices and eating habits. For most Americans, daily meals are a necessary chore—something we have to "get through" in order to have time for soccer practice, homework, laundry, PTA, Fantasy Football, or whatever we've brought home from the office. Even when we're eating foods we truly enjoy, we rarely take time to savor the experience. Time is the American nemesis. Lengthy meals with lots of social interaction are the stuff of holidays, not everyday living. For many Europeans, every good meal is still an experience.

TIP *In Europe, it is not uncommon for strangers to be seated at the same table. Traveling with a family, you're not as likely to encounter this, but it's good to be familiar with the custom.*

Most Europeans still adhere to this philosophy regarding meals—breakfast like a king, lunch like a prince, and dinner like a pauper. Meals are also a time to talk. Dinner can last for hours, so don't expect to eat and run. Slow down, relax, and join the conversation. Enjoy where you are and the culture of the surrounding town. Often you will hear someone in the street singing or playing an instrument. In Europe, ambience extends well beyond the dining room walls.

GENERAL GUIDELINES

Water

One of the most expensive commodities in Europe is water. Drinking fountains are not always available and many restrooms use water that is not suited for drinking. Often you are forced to buy bottled water. Save your bottles. When you find a place to fill them up safely, do so. A small collapsible cooler is a good investment. Ask the hotel to freeze a few bottles of water to use as ice. As they melt, you will also have cool water to drink.

Europe also has flat water and fizzy, or carbonated, water. Fizzy water is soda water and is an acquired taste. At restaurants and cafés, most people ask for bottled water. However, we found, that if we asked for table water, it was free. Table water comes in a pitcher, but don't expect ice. Unless you're in a high-end restaurant that caters to American tourists, ice is rare in Europe. Some places do have it, but most servers will give you a funny look if you ask. The first night we arrived in Frankfurt, Germany, we went to a pizza place without knowing the difference between "table water" and "bottled water." We simply asked for water. In Germany, however, water is typically fizzy unless you specifically ask for flat. The water came by the glass and was fizzy, which the kids didn't like too well. Even worse, when the bill came we realized the water cost more than the pizza!

Types of Restaurants

In some countries you will find distinct levels of restaurants. In Italy, for instance, a bar (*caffè*) is the center of social life, not a place to consume large amounts of alcohol. Italians may visit their local bar several times in the morning for coffee, return for panini at lunch and again for a cocktail in the early evening. Although alcohol is served, the main function is a café. This is where you, the American traveler, can go if you want a quick, inexpensive bite to eat. In city bars you'll find two pricing structures: *al banco* if you are sitting or standing at the bar, *à tavola* if you are seated at a table and waited on. As in

America, food that comes with full table service also comes with a hefty charge, usually two to four times what you'd pay for the same meal *al banco*. Similar to an American delicatessen, *a rosticceria* serves ready-made hot foods that you can take with you or eat at one of a few small tables. At the *rosticceria* you'll see chickens roasting on a spit in the window. The *osteria, trattoria,* and *ristorante* are all full-scale restaurants. An *osteria* traditionally serves simpler meals such as a plate of spaghetti and a glass of wine; a *trattoria* offers full meals in an informal atmosphere; and a *ristorante* is a fancier establishment with printed menus (as opposed to chalkboards), extensive wine lists, waiters in bow ties and a tab that reflects all the high-end ambience. Many smaller restaurants use the fancier names to create the allure of a more expensive restaurant with the service of the lesser ones. And, of course, what would Italy be without its *pizzeria*.

Empty Restaurants

RUN! Avoid these. One night after a visit to the Eiffel Tower we decided to eat at a charming little restaurant not far away. The absence of customers should have been a tip off. The food was poor and the service worse. Also keep in mind that travel guides are not always the best way to choose a good restaurant either. A good restaurant will be filled with locals. Listen to the language spoken in a crowded restaurant. Locals know best and their favorite spots are usually less expensive as well.

Menus

Make sure you take a *Pocket Menu Reader* with you each day. These mini-glossaries (not magnifiers) can be found at most bookstores and travel stores and come in very handy. A dictionary will tell you the French word for chicken (*poulet*). The Menu Reader gives you the correct terms for baked chicken, fried chicken, chicken in wine, and so on. If your children have a sense of adventure, translations won't matter as much. Sometimes it's fun to order *poisson* (French for fish) and then wonder how it will be prepared. There are other times however, when you wish you had asked. Just because you are in a country where English is spoken, it is not a guarantee that you know what food you're getting. Even in Britain you will be surprised by the different names of foods (bangers and mash, bubble and squeak, and mince 'n tatties are all standard dinner fare).

Tipping

More often than not, tips are included in your bill. If you leave a tip, you will have overpaid but made a lifelong friend of your server. Even in the small cafés, the tip is generally included. Restaurants in Italy also have a cover charge for the plates, silverware, bread and other basic items. This charge is also included in your bill and can add an extra $15 to $20 to the total cost. Not all restaurants have this charge (it is more common in high-tourist areas), so ask before you are seated. It's perfectly okay to walk away if there is a cover charge.

BREAKFAST

Breakfast can easily be the most economical meal. Most of the time we try to sleep at places that offer free breakfasts (Bed and Breakfasts, hotels with continental breakfast, etc.). If your lodging doesn't include breakfast, pick up some fruit and bread (butter, cheese, etc.) the night

before and create your own "continental" meal in the morning. That being said, I also have to admit that breakfast "out" in Europe is a real treat. Nearly every corner has its own pastry shop and I defy anyone to find a bad one. The smell alone will make your mouth water and pull your feet toward the door. These *patisseries, panetterie,* and *Bäckereien* are an important part of the culture, so it's good to splurge every now and then and enjoy them. Just be sure you have a money-saving plan for lunch and dinner so you don't break the budget.

LUNCH AND DINNER

Lunch for us often consisted of bread, cheese, and fruit—not, however, on the same days that we'd enjoyed that fare for breakfast. Around lunchtime, stop by a bakery and grab a few baguettes (French bread). Where there's bread, there's bound to be a cheese shop close by. Here your choices will be endless. Be sure to try some of the local favorites. A fruit stand is also likely to be nearby. For an occasional change, stop by a meat shop and pick up some hard salami. Lunch is served, money is saved!

Pizza

We have also found pizza very cheap and a wonderful meal for either lunch or dinner. Pizza in Europe is a bit different from pizza in the States. The crust is always thin and toppings are much more varied and interesting Remember the tuna? Do take a translation dictionary with you and make sure you understand each of the topping items. You will see combinations very different from what we are used to. Most of these are quite tasty, but some may be a little too out of the ordinary for kids. My kids were a little startled to see an egg in the middle of one pizza and equally surprised to find out how good it was.

Travel books caution that European pizza comes in one size—personal. That said, we found that three personal pizzas easily fed our family of six. At a cost of $4 to $8, this makes a very cheap meal and the variety of selections keeps meals interesting. You will also see Pizza Huts but I would avoid them. Their pizza is more expensive and the experience of European pizza is a treat.

Cheap Eats in Britain

Visit the local pubs. Most are suitable for families and even have family sections. The food is much cheaper and very good. If you want fast food in Britain, try the fish and chips. No trip to England is complete without a stop at a "chippy." There are regional variations on the fish and chips shop. In the North, the chips are served with brown gravy as well as vinegar and salt. The South of England finds this custom barbarous and wouldn't dream of ruining a pile of chips with gravy. Once you've tried both, you can draw your own conclusions.

Snacks

It's easy to work up an appetite sightseeing. We found that a backpack stocked with water, bread, fruit, and occasionally some hard salami, will keep hunger at bay during the day. Also take advantage of the local fast food. No, not McDonalds—food vendor stands. In Germany, we purchased one Bratwurst from a local vendor just so everyone could try it. You'll be surprised at how much a few snacks can dramatically reduce food costs when you finally sit down for a meal.

Chocolate also assuages hunger and quiets cravings. In Switzerland, we were on a quest to find bad chocolate. We were determined and went into every single chocolate shop we saw. At last we concluded that there simply is no bad chocolate in all of Switzerland! But Swiss chocolate gets very messy in a hurry. The paraffin in American chocolate slows the melting process, but European chocolate has no paraffin—one of the reasons it tastes better—so you'll need to keep it in a cool place.

To review . . .

- If you are willing to eat like a local, your food dollar will go much further.
- Carry water with you. A small collapsible cooler is also handy.
- Shared food, like pizza, goes a long way.
- Eat lunch on the go, but with European "fast food" like bread, cheese, and meats.

- Read menus posted outside restaurants to determine the best place for a sit-down meal.
- Purchase a menu reader so you know exactly what each item is.
- Make a point of trying/enjoying regional specialties. Experiencing local culture involves all the senses.

Family Favorites

PARIS Some eateries defy the stereotype. Generally prime location means premium pricing but when we're in Paris, we always visit the Caffe Le Petit-Pont, which faces Notre Dame. The food is quite reasonable and the atmosphere incredible. To sit across from this massive, ornate edifice as daylight fades and cathedral lights illuminate the building is an experience not to be missed.

FLORENCE Our favorite place here is the Gran Caffe San Marco at the San Marco Piazza. It is a wonderful, very inexpensive, family style restaurant/pizzeria with no cover charge or service charge.

ROME When in Rome, eat gelato—Italian ice cream—and eat it every day!

TRANSPORTATION
Planes, Trains and Mass Transit

## CHAPTER 5

TRANSPORTATION
Planes, Trains and Mass Transit

I think most families assume they are going to rent a car to get around. Don't lock yourself into just one idea of transportation. Do your research. There are many ways to get around once you have gotten wherever you're going. If you're staying in a city like Washington, D.C. with a wonderful transportation system and expensive parking, it makes little sense to rent a car. However, if you're like our family and always on the move to the next adventure, a rental car or van may be the best option. Often we use a combination of various modes of transportation.

In the Paris Metro (Subway)

METROPOLITAN MASS TRANSIT

Europe has a wonderful mass transit system. Nearly every large city has both an underground train (subway) and an efficient bus system, and it's far, far easier to learn these systems than to try to navigate an unfamiliar car through crowded, unfamiliar streets. In Paris or London, public transport is convenient, affordable (use multi-day or weekly passes for the best value), and far reaching. The underground can easily take you from tourist site to tourist site. From Paris, you can travel as far away as Versailles or Rueil Malmaison, home to Napoleon and

Josephine. Make sure you have a good map and be alert for pickpockets. Hold backpacks and bags on your lap.

Trains are fine for day trips but harder to manage with kids and suitcases in tow. Trains also require adherence to a strict schedule. Again, consider purchasing local or regional train passes, which can often be used for both trains and buses.

Public transportation in Europe also affords serendipitous art experiences. At a train stop, a man with an accordion may climb aboard and play until the next stop. Perhaps he'll sing as well, which is a real treat in any foreign language. Afterwards he passes the hat, but a few coins are a small price for the added ambience and the tunes stay with you the whole day. Yet another world lies under the city. Adventure awaits travelers in the tubes—everything from local art, to shopping (fashion is art), to an occasional small orchestra around the corner and just hope you have time to listen before your train arrives.

INTER-CITY TRANSPORT

The key to transportation choices may be your family's sense of adventure and the schedule you wish to keep. If your plans are focused on city sights and experiences, traveling by train from city to city is a good way to soak up a little of the countryside without the expense of a rental car. Our family, however, loves the ability to make changes as we travel and having a car allows us to do just that. If we learn about a place not too far from the beaten path, then off we go. So what if we get to the hotel a few hours later. Isn't that what phones are for? Often a side excursion becomes the most memorable point of our vacation.

Driving in Europe

This really isn't too difficult. I do recommend you have a good reference key for the various road signs, but most are easily understood. A good road atlas is also a must. And it must be current. A specialty map store near your home should have a good selection. You can also buy maps online, but some are much easier to use than others. I like to open a map up and take a good look before buying. Buy maps ahead of time to familiarize yourself with your destination areas. Later, with map in hand, locate your destination city, pick a few places in between as references, and follow the signs to the reference points until you reach your destination. Make sure you carry both your driver's license and passport with you. If you are traveling with a family throughout one or more countries, a car is often the easiest and most efficient way to go.

TIP *Be sure to buy your maps in the U.S. before you leave. If you wait until you reach your destination, you'll have trouble finding maps in English. Not a problem in London, but Brussels might be a challenge.*

Free Wheels

Yes, you can drive for free—well, almost. There are still fuel costs (and I'm working on those). Like airlines and hotel chains, rental car agencies also use points. Redeem these points for really cool stuff or get free rental days, which I think are even cooler. Most rental points don't roll over, however, so you need to use them before they expire. Rather than redeeming points for something you may never use, consider trading them for something you are trying to accumulate anyway—airline points! It's not a one-for-one exchange, but every little bit helps.

Of course the best way to use car rental points is for free rentals on vacation. Like the airlines, rental agencies have blackout dates and they have peak and off-peak periods when you get more bang for your points. It's also possible to combine free days with paid days. Not all rental plans are the same and some will only let you use points on domestic rentals, so check out your options carefully.

Another source of free transportation is the home exchange program discussed in Chapter 3. Remember this is an exchange. Use of a Land Rover in Kenya means the Land Rover's owner will be driving your Mini-Cooper in Tallahassee. Make sure you have the proper insurance coverage for both parts of the deal. Also be sure the exchange partner's vehicle will accommodate your family comfortably.

Rental Cars

Car rentals are often quite negotiable. I learned a valuable lesson from Richard Paul Evans. Always ask, "Is that the best you can do?" This works particularly well when you ask loudly enough that competing agents can hear. Even if your agent has quoted the lowest price, she may be able to upgrade you to a larger car. Or maybe you can take the price you have and shop rental counters for a better deal. Rental car reservations are not set in stone and a little counter-to-counter effort can save you some big money.

TIP *Always have a **confirmed** reservation before starting a trip. We had a reservation, but the agency hadn't confirmed the availability of a seven-passenger vehicle until we were already on our way. Because the reservation was made, we assumed it was also complete. Assumption is not a good thing when you need a seven-passenger vehicle in Europe. In the future I will also always check to see if I can do the agency a favor with a drop-off. In this case, it saved us hundreds of dollars.*

A good example of the power of negotiation occurred when we had a car rental snafu in Germany. When we arrived, neither the van we thought we had reserved nor any similar (or larger) vehicle was available. A smaller vehicle simply wouldn't work for our large family with luggage and we had the added complication of needing to return the van in Paris where our return flight originated. I began to shop rates at the counters. Most didn't have a seven-passenger vehicle available. Those who did either wouldn't allow the Paris return or wanted to charge us a tremendous drop-off fee. When I asked the Hertz agent if he could help, his first response was that he didn't have anything. But when I mentioned the Paris return, he asked me to wait a moment. It so happened that they had a seven-passenger van that had to go back to their Paris office. Now they needed us just as badly as we needed them. Earlier I had been willing to pay the going rate just to have a car. Now we began negotiations and I was able to secure a seven-passenger van for less money than a mid-size vehicle and no drop-off fee.

Insurance

Make sure you have adequate insurance. Check first with your local insurance agent. Find out what coverage is required overseas. Also keep in mind that many agencies overseas will not recognize foreign, i.e. *American*, insurance. Many rental agencies require that you purchase some sort of insurance. Traveling within the United States, I rarely pay for added coverage. Check your policy. Also check your credit card. Many companies offer insurance when their card is used for the rental.

Personally, I do not recommend relying on your own insurance when traveling abroad. I recommend you get insurance that will cover any and all circumstances. Be aware, that costs can vary greatly. Some agencies include all insurance in their rental quote. Others quote the rental without insurance and charge you an arm and leg when you pick up the car. I suggest that you only deal with rental agencies that include insurance in the price. That way there are no surprises. We have never had to use insurance abroad, but I never want to have an accident in a foreign country and not have the coverage.

Not even the best insurance covers everything. Remember that wonderful French village of Pré-en-pail? The car trouble that kept us there overnight also required some minor repairs. We had stopped in this quaint little village to refuel. Our minivan was a diesel, and I had hoped diesel would be a universal word. Well, it is not and I could find no one who spoke any English, so I began to make assumptions. My choices were gasoil and *plomb*. Both handles were green. *Gasoil* sounded more like gasoline, so I assumed *plomb* must be diesel and filled up. As soon as I turned over the engine, it began to sputter and cough. Luckily, I had seen a Peugeot garage just a block down the road. I pulled in and tried to explain what I thought I had done. After some time and a lot of hand gestures, the mechanic unscrewed the cap, inhaled deeply, and exclaimed "No!" Hoping that one of the insurances might cover this mishap; I immediately called the rental agency from the shop's phone. They assured me that no insurance covered stupidity.

Buy-Back Leases

There is also a little known program called a Buy-Back or purchase/ repurchase. What this amounts to is buying a car and then selling it back to the company at a prearranged date for a prearranged price. The price difference represents your "rental" fee, but because technically you're purchasing the vehicle, you get unlimited mileage, a car that's quite literally fresh from the showroom floor, and—usually—a much lower per-day rate than a traditional rental. Sometimes you can also get full insurance coverage at no additional cost. These programs generally require use of the car for 17 to 175 days for tourists.

For cost comparison purposes, it's important to note that these leases operate on a daily calendar, not a 24 hour one. That means if you pick up a car Saturday at noon and return it the following Saturday by noon, that counts as eight days, even though it's only seven 24 hour periods. Keep this in mind if your use time is close to either the minimum or maximum requirement.

You can arrange the purchase or lease via one of two U.S. based travel companies, either of which can price out both a lease (customized to your particular dates and needs) and a standard rental if that turns out to be cheaper. Do your homework. Shop for prices for each option. I found a very good purchase/re-purchase price for our trip to Italy, but with further searching found an even better rate on a standard rental. If you are interested in the purchase/re-purchase program, here are the places to start.

> **Auto Europe** (www.autoeurope.com) is a car rental consolidator that reps Peugeot and tends to have the cheapest rental rates as well.

> **Europe by Car** (www.europebycar.com) reps both Renault and Peugeot and does leases—only leases, and nothing but leases—so they really know their stuff.

If you prefer to go directly to the sources, you can get more information on the Renault leasing program at www.renaultusa.com. The Peugeot program is at www.peugeot-openeurope.com.

Factory Purchases

If you're making an extended visit to your destination usually more than five weeks, consider purchasing a vehicle outright. This may sound like a bit of a commitment but if you're already planning to purchase a European car, buying it at the source can actually save you money. Like most aspects of economic travel, this takes planning and negotiation. Some folks have even purchased a new car from the factory in Germany and negotiated the shipping to their local dealer in the States after driving it around Europe for several weeks. Please note that not all foreign cars can be imported into the U.S. so make sure your vacation car meets all U.S. importation requirements.

TRAVEL BETWEEN COUNTRIES

The best and least expensive way to travel between countries is a little-known secret called Ryanair (www.Ryanair.com), the king of discount travel. Ryanair has a new large fleet of Boeing 737-800 series aircraft and uses smaller, less busy airports to reduce fees and the savings are incredible. A one-way fare from London (Stansted Airport) to Milan, Italy (Bergamo Airport) has been as low as $10. Taxes and fees are often more than the airfare. Even with taxes and fees you still can fly from London to Milan for around $60 or round trip from Paris (Beauvais) to Rome (Ciampino) for about $50. Just like discount airlines in the United States, these low fares have forced the major airlines to reduce their rates, which benefits all travelers.

After our trip to Italy, our two oldest children flew from Rome to Paris to visit friends before flying home. The total cost was $22 each. Check the Web sites to see if it pays to fly into a city a bit off the beaten track or use one of the major airlines.

Additional sites detailing similar programs include www.searchlowestfares.com, www.easyjet.com, www.wegolo.com, www.applefares.com, www.openjet.com and www.skyscanner.net. If you are flying to Eastern Europe, try www.skyeurope.com or www.wizzair.com.

Ryanair's cheapest fares are available to people traveling during off-peak periods. Generally the weekend fares are higher than the midweek fares. The cheapest fares require an advance purchase of at least fourteen days, in some case twenty-eight days. The cheapest fares are also discounted automatically for Internet sales, so visit www.Ryanair.com to check out the savings. Look at the specials. There are airfares as low as $2 plus taxes and fees, even some free destinations. There are even discounts for airport parking and hotel rooms through Ryanair.

In order to receive these unbelievably low fares, you must book well in advance and be flexible with respect to your city of departure. If you want to fly from Germany to Rome for a day or two, you can only fly out of Frankfurt (Hahn). Despite the low fares, Ryanair is not for everyone. However, if your travel plans include flights within Europe, it's definitely worth checking out their site. With a little planning and flexibility, you can fly around Europe very cheaply.

TIP *These are no-frills airlines to the extreme. Take your own beverage, and keep your luggage to a minimum or expect to pay a surcharge for bags over twenty kilograms (44 pounds).*

There is nothing better than debarking from a free flight, hopping into a free car, and heading to your free hotel. That is what I call a vacation!

To review . . .

- Drive free with points from previous rentals.
- Negotiate the rental price whether you reserve online or by phone. Then negotiate again at the counter.
- See if you can do the rental company a favor. Use that as leverage to lower your cost.
- Negotiate a car with your home exchange.
- Buy a car using the purchase/re-purchase plan
- If you have a "base camp," you may not need a car. Use local transportation. Buy a pass.
- If traveling long distances or to other countries, consider a discount airline. It may be cheaper.

Family Favorites

We have used RyanAir many times and love it. Make sure you know the restrictions.

SIGHTSEEING

Night (and Day) at the Museum

## CHAPTER 6

SIGHTSEEING
Night (and Day) at the Museum

Driving to Freiberg, Germany, we were hungry and a bit travel weary. Noticing a sign for a *berg* (castle), we grabbed a few things at a bakery and headed in the direction indicated. We ate our meal at castle ruins dating back to 1025, nearly a thousand years old. It was an absolutely fantastic experience and aside from the cost of food that we would have bought anyway, absolutely free.

As I mentioned earlier, our family travels to explore. What we choose to explore may be different from what your family chooses. That's okay. You can't do it all, so do what best suits the interests of your family. Popular tourist attractions can also be big budget-busters. Certainly you will want to see some of them, but our experience has shown that the things we find to do for free are often more memorable. Remember that what you *do* creates longer lasting memories than what you simply see or hear.

FREE OR NEARLY SO

When you arrive in a city or town, go straight to the Tourist Board Information Center. You'll find them everywhere, from large cities like

London and Paris to the small towns. Gather as much information as you can about places to stay and eat cheaply. Even if you don't need or use the information this trip, it's a great reference for the next time. Get information on festivals, parks, concerts, and places of interest that are free. We also discovered a great Web site, www.freetodo.freeserve.co.uk, that lists free things to do all over Europe.

Public Places

Churches, public parks and buildings, and college campuses can be relaxing, informative, and awe-inspiring places to visit. On a trip to England, visits to both Cambridge and Oxford included informal walks through the grounds of their respective universities.

Local lakes, beaches and pools are relaxing, fun, and frequently free, or very inexpensive. Here is a list of just a few of the many public places available.

> **Churches:** Coventry Cathedral, England; Castle Church, Martin Luther/Wittenberg, Germany; nearly any church in Rome
>
> **Parks:** Kensington Gardens, London; Parc des Buttes-Chaumont, Paris; Villa Borghese, Rome
>
> **Public Buildings:** Roman Forum, Rome; Chilehaus, Hamburg, Germany; castle ruins—UK, Germany, France, Slovakia, etc.

Local Celebrations

From New Orleans' Mardi Gras to Swiss Days in tiny Midway, Utah, every town has some sort of celebration or festival reflecting its heritage or natural environment. Find out ahead of time when festivals are happening (those city tourist boards mentioned above have Web sites as well as offices) and try to plan your visit at that time. Fourth of July celebrations are held in most every city and town across the United States. Small town parades and fireworks are great fun and wonderful for very young children, but Independence Day celebrations in Boston or Washington, D.C. are major entertainment events that will leave older children with unforgettable memories.

In Europe, even the very small villages have some kind of festival. The majority of these are held during the spring and summer, but in some Alpine villages, it's the winter carnivals that you don't want to miss. It seems like the Europeans love an excuse to party in the streets, and party they do. From Beer Fests (just about anywhere in Germany) to the Cheese Rolling of Cooper's Hill (Gloucester, England) to local festivals celebrating the return of a lost lamb or child, you can have an incredible day without breaking the budget. Another one of our favorite things to do is read about the history of an area or a person from that area before going there. When we visit the relevant historical sites, our "book learning" gains another dimension of reality. After we learned about Joan of Arc, for example, we traveled from her birthplace in Orleans (south of

Paris) to Rouen, where she was burned at the stake.

Most of these historical sites are free and provide a hands-on experience that children simply can't get from books alone.

In Italy, historic hill towns are wonderful to explore. Assisi, famous for St. Francis, is one of our favorites. Explore the castle that has protected the city since 1174.

Visit the Church where St. Francis is entombed. Be prepared for the breathtaking view of the city as you approach. Pictures cannot do it justice.

La Rocca Maggiore (Castle) watching over Assisi, Italy

Places you visit for free offer guilt-free pleasure. Seasoned travelers frequently note that it's not the tourist attractions that make a trip; it's enjoying the everyday aspects of local culture. Whether it's swimming in crystal Alpine lakes, walking Boston's Freedom Trail, or enjoying a plowman's lunch in a Welsh pub, it's all wonderful and it's all free.

MONEY-SAVING STRATEGIES

Discounts

When the price of individual admissions becomes too hefty a sum, consider purchasing a yearly family pass. There are two advantages to this—first, you save on your initial purchase and, if there's opportunity and interest, you've got free admission for the second visit. Also ask for family

discounts. While visiting the Island of Elba we wanted to see where Napoleon lived. The tickets were quite expensive and no family pass was available. We asked if they would make an exception and, after some deliberation, they agreed to let all seven of us in for the cost of two parents and one child. It never hurts to ask and frequently pays off quite well.

And if your sister is willing to pay you enough, you might even slip into Napoleon's tub for a quick picture. (I wonder if Napoleon had a rubber ducky?)

If you happen to be traveling in Vienna, you can enjoy truly outstanding opera even on a tight budget. Ninety minutes before each performance, 600 standing-room tickets go on sale for as little as €2 (about $3). Opera buffs are happy to stand for a few hours to hear the world's best voices; non-opera buffs often buy the cheap tickets just to explore the public rooms of the Opera House and slip out before the overture begins. Guided tours of the building range from $5.50 to $10, so the standing room ticket is a great deal for everyone.

Popular museums like the Louvre, Orsay and Uffizi often have reduced price days and/ or free admission for children on certain days. To know this information you need to get a good guidebook (we use Rick Steves' books and the *Lonely Planet* series). These list costs and daily schedules. You can also ask at the front desk of your hotel. (If you are not staying in a hotel, just pick one and ask.)

Sometimes when it is close to closing, places of interest offer reduced rates, or even a free visit. While vacationing in New England we stopped at an aquarium near the end of the day. When my

wife explained that we had four children who would love to look inside for just a few moments, the manager let us in for free to see the last sea lion show. On our way to the show we saw many of the other animals as well.

TIP *Not all museums are ideal for children. We found this to be the case while visiting the Accademia Museum in Florence, which features classic sculptures including Michelangelo's David. There are other works of art, however, which may make children quite uncomfortable. Admission to the Accademia is about $10. It is rather small and its main attraction is the David statue. A full replica is on display in the plaza for free, and you can even take pictures of the replica.*

Altered Expectations

No one wants to miss quintessential landmarks like the Eiffel Tower or the Leaning Tower of Pisa. Unfortunately, these places can empty your wallet in a hurry. Check to see if there's an alternate way to get at least some of the experience for less money. At the Eiffel Tower, for example, you can ride the elevators all the way to the top, or you can take the stairs to the mid-section. The view from the mid-section is quite amazing, and the difference in cost is substantial. (I will admit, however, that the view from the top at night, when both the tower and Paris are all lit up, is breathtaking.)

Many places can be enjoyed without going in. Such is the case with the Leaning Tower of Pisa. The cost to climb the tower is about $30 per person (that's nearly $200 for our family). We chose instead to pile into a horse-drawn carriage for $30 (total cost) and take a personal tour of the city. We still saw the tower, and we saw a whole lot more as well for a fraction of the cost.

JUSTIFIABLE EXTRAS

Of course, some sites and activities are well worth the extra money; just choose carefully based on your own priorities (ours are culture and learning). A few experiences are even worth paying extra for. If you are going to visit the Coliseum in Rome, for example, you may want to consider

spending another $5 to get a personal tour from a gladiator. Not only does the tour include a free photo with him (a $10 to $15 cost if purchased alone), you also get to bypass the lines - and you hear a fascinating history lesson to boot.

During peak season, long lines are also common for popular sites like the Louvre. You can avoid these by ordering tickets online or by telephone. There is a service charge, but the value of time saved may well be worth it.

SOUVENIRS

On vacation, even the cheapest trinkets can seem irresistible. Learn to limit yourself—many souvenirs are lost or broken before you get home. Others survive the journey but eventually become bookshelf dust-collectors. Choose useful items that you will treasure. Whenever we look at the Nottingham lace valences in our bedroom windows, we are reminded of our wonderful adventure in the land of Robin Hood.

Our children collect rocks wherever we go. They have found some incredible ones, including gems from the Swiss Alps. Not only are these souvenirs free, they also generate memories of experiences rather than images of gift shops. (We also have salt from the salt mines of Berchtesgaden, Germany. Not the free sample you get at the end of the tour, but actual salt from the walls of the mine. Again, the "mining" experience isn't likely to be forgotten.)

Also look for souvenirs that are produced locally, visiting the productions sites if possible. All too often the items available in little shops or vendors' carts are only replicas made far from the area you are visiting. A friend of mine visiting the Middle East purchased a beautifully decorated

Marissa's ready

The salt mines, Berchtesgaden – Germany

traditional garment, only to later find a small, obscure tag reading "Made in China." Ask if the item is produced in the region. If so, find out more about it and where it is made. In Venice, we noticed a lot of Murano glass and Burano lace. We learned that these islands were not far away and accessible with our waterbus pass.

On the island of Murano, we found plenty of wonderful shops and none of the tourist crowds. The shop owners were charming and their prices incredible. Items selling for $30 and $40 in Venice were $7 to $15 at the source. Some craftsmen are even willing to make special order items. Our favorite shop owner sold us some incredible, one-of-a kind necklaces and earrings for under $10 apiece. Murano is also known for its beaded necklaces, and our shopkeeper friend showed us how they were made and how the craft has been perfected over the years. This kind of souvenir shopping is an adventure in itself, so be sure to allow lots of time.

PHOTOS AND VIDEOS

Be sure to shoot lots of videos and still photos. I recommend using a digital camera and buying a large capacity memory card. Then, click away. At night, review the day's pictures and delete the ones that didn't turn out. Once you're home, you can have prints made of whichever shots you want and store the rest on a disk or use them as a screensavers. If your memory card gets too full before you get home, go to an internet café and upload your pictures to www. smugmug.com. This site offers unlimited photo storage space for $30 a year. Be sure you take your camera-to-computer cable!

TIP *Another option for preserving and displaying photos is a digital frame. Pictures rotate through at whatever speed you select, and it's fun to have the memories always conveniently available.*

The best video is also digital. The magic of digital video is the ease of editing. Once the editing is done, burn the video onto a DVD, which is easier to use. It's also easy to make copies so that all your children have their own memory "albums" when they leave the nest.

To review . . .

- Choose activities based on your own family's priorities.

- Seek out local festivals and public parks and buildings for interesting and inexpensive experiences.

- Use the Internet and travel guidebooks to find discounts—and don't be afraid to ask at the venue itself.

- Limit souvenirs and try to buy items produced locally.

- Use digital technology for photos and video.

- Have fun. Be flexible and open to new opportunities.

Family Favorite:

One of our favorite places to visit is the Loire Valley in Central France. We stayed in the town of Tours, where we were surrounded by more than a dozen chateaux (castles), including Chateau D'Amboise (home of Leonardo da Vinci) and Chateau Chenonceau (Catherine de Medici). While Tours has been described as the most convenient and least appealing of the Loire Valley cities, it is places like Tours that offer the best pricing on hotels and easy access to the beautiful countryside. From there you can roam from chateau to chateau, reliving history at every turn. The cost of guided castle tours is rather minimal, around $5 for adults and $3 for kids.

If the kids are up to it, and you are a little more adventurous, you can explore the chateaux and vineyards along the Loire River by bicycle. The government recently completed 500 miles of sign-posted cycling paths and bike-friendly minor roads through the Loire Valley. For more information on local bike rental operations and downloadable itineraries for bike trips of less than an hour to a week or more, visit loire-a-velo.fr, or contact the Loire Valley Travel office at Loire.Valley.Travel@wanadoo.fr.

CHAPTER SEVEN

WHAT TO TAKE

Eeeny, Meeny, Miney, or Joe

WHAT TO TAKE

Eeeny, Meeny, Miney, or Joe

What you choose to pack may be as varied as the destinations available, but following just a few simple rules will limit confusion and help maintain your sanity. Remember, you have to lug all this stuff around. And after you've loaded everything into the rental car, will there still be room for the kids? (Actually, most rental car agencies have printed recommendations regarding luggage capacity. Look on their website or ask. Most of the times the bags, if packed right, will fit in the back; the backpacks may have to ride on laps.)

CLOTHING AND PERSONAL ITEMS

No matter where we go or how long we will be gone, we have made it a rule that everyone is allowed one 22 inch expandable pull-behind suitcase and one school backpack or daypack. (Did I just hear gasps from the female contingent of your family?) We have spent a month in Europe using this rule.

Take just enough clothing for a week. Most items can be worn at least twice before laundering, and I have yet to visit a country without a laundromat. Spending half a day doing laundry can actually be a welcome relief after several days of perpetual motion. It's a great time to sit down and tackle that stack of postcards you've collected but haven't had time to write. Note: If you are going to pack around dirty clothes, be sure to either roll them very tightly or, better yet, invest in a travel bag that removes the air—a great space saver.

Plan and pack ahead

Well before our trip my wife makes a list of what each person needs. About a week before the trip, she lines the suitcases up in the living room and begins packing. As she does this, she checks each item off the list. A sweater and a light jacket are just as warm as a heavy coat and easier to pack. (You can save even more space by wearing the jacket on the plane.) Choose seasonal clothing, but remember that weather changes so always take jeans as well. If you are going to take umbrellas, take the smaller ones. A high-quality jacket with a hood is often just as good as a cheap umbrella. The key is to pack lightly. You really don't need that much.

TIP: *Make sure your expandable suitcase starts out <u>un</u>expanded. This way you know there will be room to bring your souvenir treasures home. Baggage restrictions don't change on the return flight.*

Electronics

Don't forget your camera and video camera. Throw a small flashlight in your camera bag "just in case." Make sure you have electrical converters for all the countries you are going to visit. When choosing hair dryers, curling irons and shavers, make sure they are dual voltage. Some operate within a range of voltage that is acceptable in *all* countries, but be sure to read all the small print before purchasing. It may be cheaper to buy new appliances with dual converters built in than to purchase a separate converter. Purchase good quality converters - cheap ones often don't work well or for long, and once you're out of the United States it's very difficult to buy one that converts U.S. voltage. I recommend carrying all bathroom items, hair dryers, curling irons makeup, etc. in one smaller pull-behind.

Backpacks

During the flight, backpacks are for personal items like video games, CD players, notebooks, reading material, snacks, etc. Once you reach your destination it's not necessary that everyone have his or hers with them all the time. Use just one or two backpacks as you explore. Keep snacks, water, translation books, maps, and such in them. If you have children under five, a small collapsible stroller is a lifesaver. Secure a luggage tag on it and check it with your bags.

TIP: *You can also take one additional larger pull-behind for shoes, the miscellaneous items mentioned above, and souvenirs. We have also used the extra space to pack a queen-size blowup bed, pump and sheets.*

Car seats

If there are preschoolers in your family, it's wise to take a child seat with you for both the plane and the rental car. The FAA strongly recommends that children weighing less than forty pounds be put into a child restraint system appropriate for their weight. Children under the age of two may be carried on the lap of an adult, but the lap child should have some kind of restraint. If you don't take a child seat on the plane, make sure you reserve one with your rental. Some car seats can double as a stroller; convenience may justify the extra expense.

PASSPORTS & VALUABLES

If you are traveling out of the country, it is important to get everyone's passports early. There are new restrictions, and delays are common. I suggest having passports at least six months before departure. It usually takes a month or two to get them. (If you need a passport quickly, you can use sites such as www.passportsandvisas.com and www.americanpassport.com for 24 hour service.) Also well ahead of time, check to be sure you have enough blank pages in your passport. Some countries require at least two blank passport pages to enter. If you need additional pages, send your current passport to the passport center; there is no

TIP: *Children's passports expire in just five years; be sure to check the date well in advance of your travel.*

TIP: *Email your itinerary, including flights, hotels, and confirmation numbers, to yourself and a family member. You might also include driving instructions to hotels and other destinations. If any of these are lost or stolen all the information is just an internet café click away.*

charge for this service. For extended vacations, check the country's visa requirements. Typically, you won't need one for stays less than 90 days, but never assume.

We make color copies of all our passports, the front and back of each credit card, driver's license and birth certificate; then we keep these in a waist belt "in case any of these items are lost or stolen." Parents should be in charge of all passports at all times. If you are driving from country to country, you may be stopped at the border and asked for documentation, so keep everything handy. Once you're home again, shred these copies or store them in a secure place like a safe deposit box.

Money

Our recommendation is to not exchange your money in the United States. You will pay excessive fees and get a poor rate of exchange. At the most, take a few $100 traveler's checks for emergencies. You may wish to exchange just a small amount at the airport, for taxies or other necessary incidentals. Keep in mind that exchange booths will exchange at a higher rate. If you want a quick reference to carry with you, go to www.oanda.com/convert/cheat sheet. Pick your currency and print out a nice wallet-size conversion chart. If you have a Blackberry or other PDA, you can get free conversion software on the Internet; be sure to update it right before you leave.

We find it cheaper to purchase items with our credit card and let it do the conversion without fees. If there's a chance you'll need the card for cash advances, get a pin number. Remember that banks often charge interest at a higher rate, and from day one, for cash advances. To avoid these, prepay with money you have saved or pay off the amount as soon as you get home. You can also set up a specific account with funds to draw on rather than using your regular account or credit card. Plan ahead—if you end up paying interest on an inexpensive vacation, it is no longer inexpensive.

Also be wary of fees when you use your ATM card. Fees for withdrawing money from an ATM that is not your bank can be even higher outside the United States. Ask your bank for a list of institutions that can process your card without fees.

Waist Belts

Waist belts are good for carrying valuables. Make sure they are well hidden under a shirt or blouse that has been tucked in. Don't try to use the waist belt like a wallet, accessing it for every little purchase. Instead, keep enough money for incidentals in your pocket and the majority of cash or traveler's checks in the waist belt. Both parents should have a waist belt, one with the original passports and half the cash and traveler's checks, and the other with passport copies and the rest of the money. Each adult also keeps one credit card and his or her own driver's license. This way, if one waist belt is lost and stolen, you haven't lost everything.

TIP: *You can also take one additional larger pull-behind for shoes, the miscellaneous items mentioned above, and souvenirs. We have also used the extra space to pack a queen-size blowup bed, pump and sheets.*

Leave wallets at home. Keep some money in a pocket and your license and one credit card in your waist belt. If you insist on bringing one, fasten a safety pin across the opening of your pocket from the inside, making it possible—but difficult—to pull the wallet out. This reduces the likelihood of losing it to a pickpocket.

TIP: *We have had a couple experiences with pickpockets. One was successful, but the more interesting one was a failed attempt. In Paris, on what our youngest refers to as Anastasia's bridge, a lady made an attempt at picking my pocket. A poor attempt, but an attempt nonetheless. The ploy is this: someone will approach you with a map and ask for help. While distracting you with the map, the hand under the map goes into your pocket and your money disappears. Luckily for us, the woman was very bad at her trade. I felt her hand and slapped it away. My wife and children thought I was quite rude until I told them what had transpired. The interesting thing is that when we re-crossed the bridge, the would-be thief waved to us and smiled. It was very strange.*

To review . . .

- Pack light - a week's worth of clothes is sufficient.
- Pack all electronics, shoes, etc. in a separate carry-on.
- Allow plenty of time to secure passports.
- Carry copies of passports and other documents.
- Use a credit card to avoid high conversion rates.
- Leave wallets at home; use a waist belt instead.

PACKING LIST:

Make a master list of all the items that you need on your computer - One for domestic travel and one for foreign travel.

Basic items/suitcase:

- Clothing
  - Shirts
  - Slacks, jeans, shorts, etc
  - Underwear & socks
  - Jacket or sweatshirt (depending on weather conditions)
- Toiletry kit
- Small first-aid kit
- Medication/prescriptions
- Extra glasses/contacts
- Address list (to send postcards)
- Camera, battery, film, lenses, bag
- Video Camera
- Shoes

- Fanny pouch (eliminates need for purse)
- Expandable bag
- Blow up mattress & sheets
- Copies of your documents

Backpack items (for the plane and/or car ride):

- Guidebook and travel information
- Money
  - Travelers checks
  - Debit card (ATM card)
  - No more than 2 Credit Cards
  - A few personal Checks
  - Cash
- Needed documents
  - Airline tickets
  - Driver's License and/or Passport
  - Student ID's
  - Insurance details
  - Car rental confirmation/receipt
  - Journal
  - Note pad/pen
- Zip-lock bags (great for seashells and rocks collected, dirty diapers, and just about everything else)
- Extra Batteries
- Water bottle (empty if flying)
- Medication needed on flight/ride
- Few toiletries to freshen up
- Snacks to tide you over (gum/mints)
- Anti-bacterial hand wipes or wash

For overseas travel:

- Passport & Visa (if required)
- Rail pass voucher
- Electronic adaptors for the country or region you are visiting

Extra items for youth and children's backpacks:

- Gameboy or other electronic game
- Small compact games such as Phase 10, Uno, etc.
- Small books about the places they will visit
- A good reading book
- Colored pencils/crayons
- Coloring book and/or paper
- Wet wipes
- Personal MP3 or tape player

Items for babies:

- Folding stroller
- Diaper bag—diapers, treats, bottles, toys, bibs, extra pacifiers, blanket, zip-lock bags, change of clothing, jacket/sweater

Having the items you need helps you relax and enjoy the trip more.

CHAPTER EIGHT

GLUE STICKS,
VELCRO and DUCT TAPE
Keeping it All Together

GLUE STICKS, VELCRO & DUCT TAPE
Keeping it All Together

Vacationing with kids presents both unique challenges and amazing rewards. Some days you wonder if you should have left the kids behind and headed off with just your spouse. But there are also times when you see delight in your children's eyes, hear insight in their comments and genuine interest in their questions, and realize that they are truly beginning to understand the world around them. Hopefully, the more that children travel, the more they appreciate both the things they have and what the rest of the world has to offer.

In this chapter we've gathered things we've learned that make various aspects of family travel a little easier, safer, or more fun.

GET KIDS INVOLVED EARLY

Prior to each vacation, my wife assigns each child a report to be completed before the actual trip. These assignments relate to either the geographic area we are visiting or a famous person connected with that region. This assignment should not be given on the trip, because that has a tendency to take some of the fun out of the experience. As you travel, simply pointing out the places and how they relate to what has been studied brings life to the trip and makes it more interesting. We have been amazed at the things our kids have told us about a place. NOTE: We

TIP: *Assignments of a different kind are a good idea after you reach your destination. Have one or two children in charge of backpacks, another looking for places to fill up water bottles, and so on.*

home school our kids, so these types of assignments are nothing out of the ordinary for them. If you can't imagine using the words *vacation* and *report* or *assignment* in the same sentence when talking to your children, don't give up the idea—just spend some time thinking of a more appropriate way to present it. Despite their protestations, kids do enjoy learning.

FLY HEALTHY

Hydrate

Drink at least 8 to 12 ounces of water each hour that you are on the plane. Avoid drinking alcohol and caffeine as these increase dehydration. Apply moisturizing lotion to as much of your body as possible; re-apply as needed to minimize the dehydration of your skin. (Remember to continue drinking water after you arrive. Also take a shower or bath to help re-hydrate and refresh your body.)

Exercise

Walk around the cabin to exercise your limbs and stretch your muscles. On long flights there's typically a video that shows ways to promote circulation. These activities will also help keep your stress levels low. Start moving as soon as you get off the plane. If possible, walk around barefoot (or at least without shoes; the stimulation is a great reviver). Stand in direct sunlight for 10-20 minutes without glasses.

Rest

Try to sleep on the plane if your flight arrives in the morning. Bring an eye mask, neck rest, slippers, earplugs or anything that will help you fall asleep. Most airlines have these items available if you ask. Avoid taking sleeping pills, however. These put you in a comatose state with little or no natural body movement. Because your blood isn't circulating as well, clotting can occur, even if you've never had any previous problems.

Finally, some sleep aids are variants of antihistamines, which tend to increase dehydration.

If your flight arrives in the evening, make every effort to stay awake. Keep yourself busy doing anything - reading, working on your laptop, or getting to know the person next to you.

Maintain a Positive Mental State

When you take off, set your watch to your destination time zone to get your mind thinking in that new time frame. Visualize your arrival and first day activities. Try to keep your mind off the time difference and don't think about what time it is at home. To reduce fatigue from cabin noise, listen to your favorite music. Bring your own, or choose one of the airline's offerings. Keep your mind alert with puzzles in the in-flight magazine (or, again, bring your own favorites).

Reduce Jet Lag

Jet lag can be a problem. Experts say our bodies need a day of adjustment for every hour of change. That thought alone is daunting if you've flown from Seattle to Paris for just a few days of vacation. You may arrive at your destination at 9 a.m. and your body is telling you it's time for bed, which is very difficult. Knowing this, folks optimistically say they'll sleep on the plane during the long flight over the ocean. However, this rarely happens. Kids love the airplane experience and are usually up the whole flight. This may be fine for them, but it's tough on the parents. Another problem is that most hotels don't allow check-in until mid-afternoon. So what do you do?

One of the fastest ways to combat jet lag is to operate on the new time as soon as possible. Eat when the locals eat; go to bed when they go to bed. When you arrive it takes some time to gather your luggage and get the rental car. If you're staying at a hotel, drive there first and ask if it's possible to check in early. If so, get settled and nap for just two or three hours. Do not sleep a long time, just enough to take the edge off. Set an alarm if necessary. If early check-in is unavailable, visit a few local sights. Take it easy; do some window shopping and get acquainted with your new city. Locate the closest subway station, local restaurants and pastry shops, or maybe pick up a phone card. When you check in later that afternoon, take a very short nap. *It's important that you go to bed at the new time the very first evening.* It will be hard to wake the kids up, so have them take a shower. The faster you can get them accustomed to the new bed time, the quicker you beat the jet lag feeling.

Another approach is to start adjusting your own internal clock by one hour each day *before* you leave. This is sometimes hard with kids, but if you get to the new time before you leave it will make your first days abroad much easier. For some helpful hints and a calculator to help adjust to the time, try this cool site: www.bodyclock.com.

BLEND IN

Some might suggest that you dress your kids in bright shirts or matching outfits to keep track of them. Though this may have worked for the Von Trapp family, it is not recommended when you are traveling abroad today. The more you look like a tourist, the more you will be treated like one. You become an easier mark for those who wish to prey.

So how do you keep everyone together? Use the buddy system. Each older child should have a younger child to keep track of. Be alert — don't let ambience get the better of your common sense. Do not let any child or teenager wander off alone. Every city has good and bad neighborhoods. Ask at the clerk at the hotel if you have questions; front desk personnel are very helpful in steering you in the right direction. If you are on a train or a bus and a child wants to sit in the upper level, all of you must do so.

Avoid "Cabin Fever" in the Car

Sometimes you spend much more time together in a car than you anticipated. It seems like you should be able to traverse a small county like England in no time, but in reality it takes quite a bit longer. For one thing, the smaller roads rarely go in a straight line, which keeps the scenery interesting but makes the ride much longer. Make sure you have things to keep kids busy. Give a child a good road map and appoint him or her the official navigator. Play Car Bingo with country- or region-specific words or pictures. Or play "Twenty Questions" relevant to information from those pre-assigned reports. Even the Alphabet Game can be a challenge in a foreign country. Be careful, however, not to completely distract children - you want them to remember the landscape as well as the in-car activities.

Balance travel and sightseeing. Know your destination, but leave enough time to visit places along the way. We try to get out of the hotel no later than 9 a.m. and leave as much of the day open as possible. You never know when you will come upon a wonderful find, and "discovery breaks" make the day much more enjoyable. The important thing is to

have fun and not stress. Once, when we found ourselves with a fair amount of waiting time before our English tour of the Neuschwanstein Castle, we rented (very cheaply) paddleboats on the nearby lake. What an experience to see the castle from this new vantage point. And we cooled down a little playing in the lake.

Learn the lingo

Language isn't usually a problem in major cities, but some of the best travel experiences occur in the towns and villages. Take a good, basic pocket dictionary with you, but also learn a few essential phrases before you go. Numbers and names of familiar foods (bread or fish, for example) are important, as well as the ability to

TIP: *If you are in a non-English speaking country and plan on visiting a castle (or other landmark) that offers tours in English, try to find out ahead of time when these tours are; then build your schedule around that activity.*

ask for restrooms. Also learn how to ask for help. Take a small notebook for drawing pictures, and think of what body language you might use to get certain ideas across. Even in places where no English is spoken, you can get by if you try.

Obviously, it's easier to learn a language when you're immersed in it. Our oldest daughter went to Germany a month before the rest of the family. She stayed with some very good friends there who were to be our host family. We were amazed at the amount of German she was able to understand by the time we arrived. She learned quickly mainly because she had to. Keep in mind, however, that - as a tourist - just because you're in a non-English speaking country doesn't mean you're truly immersed in the language. More than 90% percent of the time you will be conversing with your own family. If you really want to learn the language quickly, speak it all the time among the family while there. Even before you go, have days where family members converse only in the language of the country you're planning to visit. It's hard but well worth it.

I wrote earlier that we love to stay with families. Host families are a wonderful resource for ideas on where to eat and what to see. They can point you in directions no guidebook will ever mention, and you will gain more insight into the people and their culture. If we are traveling in the country where one of our exchange students lives, we stop to visit the family and take their son or daughter with us. This gives us a wonderful translator and makes for a more delightful trip. The experience rises to a whole new level when you are with someone who knows the area.

UNDERSTAND LOCAL CUSTOMS AND TRADITIONS

Sometimes it's the little things that bother us - sharing a café table with strangers or maybe taking the wrong turn. Try to remember that these little idiosyncrasies are part of the cultural experience. If everything was the same as Hometown, USA, what would be the point of traveling? Two somewhat significant cultural differences are discussed below. As you travel, you can add other experiences to the list.

Grocery Shopping

Anticipate differences, large grocery stores are not in every big city outside the US. Most people purchase the day's food that day, shopping at several specialty stores to do this: meat at the butcher's, bread at the bakery, and so forth. If you are staying in an exchange home or other place where you can fix your own meals, you need to plan ahead. Refrigerators are relatively small, and perishable foods such as vegetables are best purchased fresh. Store hours are also different. We have grown used to 24 hour access, but most European shops close at six or seven. Europe is also ahead of the U.S. in "green" shopping—if you don't bring a bag for groceries, you will need to purchase one. In a Salzburg grocery store, I suggested to my wife that she pack up the items to help keep the line moving. She had just begun filling a sack when the sales lady grabbed her hand, making it very clear that my wife had not paid for the bag. The situation was a bit embarrassing, but we learned an important lesson. Save bags when you shop; you can use them over and over again.

Swimming Attire

Generally, Europeans are much less bothered by nudity than Americans. That difference is most obvious on the beaches or at any swimming place. Earlier I mentioned that our daughter had traveled to Germany a month before the rest of the family. We arrived in August, and it was very hot. Our host family suggested we all go to a local lake to swim and cool off. On the way, our daughter told her mom, "Don't worry, I warned the boys". My wife wondered why our boys needed a warning. Apparently it is very common throughout Europe for women and girls to swim topless. We knew this was true on the beaches of the French Riviera but didn't realize the custom extended to small German villages. Our biggest fear was that our twelve year-old son might end up rudely staring, mouth wide open, at some woman sunbathing on the beach. Once we prepared the children, however, there seemed to be little problem.

Choice of bathing attire is also not governed by age, fitness, or body type. Remind children just to focus on having a good time without worrying about other folks' clothing choices. Europeans probably think Americans are far too uptight about these things. It's just cultural perspective.

STAY IN TOUCH

Europe offers several different types of phone cards, available at kiosks (newspaper stands) in city centers. Get the card best suited to the type of calling you are going to do. Most pay phones use a "chip" card that electronically provides information automatically once you slide it in. The problem with the chip card is that a few pay phones do not accept

it *and* it doesn't work in a private home. Calling cards that use a toll-free calling number are less convenient (you have to manually type in all the information and numbers), but they can be used anywhere. Rates vary widely, from six cents to more than two dollars per minute. Ask for the best rate to the United States if calls home are the primary intended use. If you expect to do a lot of calling within Europe, ask about those rates as well before making a decision.

Now that Europe uses the Euro, many cards can be used in multiple locations, but different rates may apply. I took my laptop on our last trip and was able to use a calling card to connect to the Internet for emails. If you're going to use your laptop, make sure you have all the telephone adapters needed for each country. You can also pre-purchase phone cards online, but the best deals will be generally found at your destination. Pay phones can accept credit cards, but the rates are typically higher and the calling process more difficult.

With today's cell phone technology, you may be able to take your current cell phone with you. Before you travel, talk to your service provider to pre-arrange a special rate for a specific time period. Otherwise you will incur exorbitant roaming charges. This may be the cheapest way to go. If your current phone will not work in Europe, your service provider can, for a fee, provide a different phone with the same number. This way, people can reach you easily if there are any problems at home. It also is very handy when you are lost or late or need to change a hotel reservation.

TIP: *Some cell phone cards look just like regular phone cards, but these can only be used on cell phones. Kiosks will not take them back, even if unopened, so be sure you know what you're buying before you leave the kiosk.*

To review . . .

- Before you travel, find a way to get kids familiar with people, places, and customs associated with the countries you will visit.
- Don't be a flight zombie. Stay hydrated, get some exercise, and consciously rest or remain alert, depending on your arrival time.
- Don't succumb to jet lag; there are steps you can take to lessen the effects of long flights.
- Don't look like a tourist.
- Balance travel and sightseeing time.
- Learn basic phrases in the local language, and carry a good pocket dictionary.
- Be respectful of local customs; you don't have to agree, but don't complain or "preach" either.
- Plan ahead in order to have easy contact with folks at home.

SAFETY

Knowing is Half the Battle

## CHAPTER 9

SAFETY
Knowing is Half the Battle

Safety is the number one concern of any parent traveling with children. We all fear that after some brief distraction (buying tickets, checking a map or bus schedule), we'll look around and realize someone is missing. Quick, what was he wearing? How was her hair combed? This is, of course, the worst-case scenario (but still every parent's nightmare).

In this modern age of digital cameras and camera cell phones, an accurate description of each person in your party should no longer be an issue. Take a picture of your children each morning; if necessary, the photo can be downloaded to a local authority's computer or emailed on the spot. Of course, you hope you'll never need that picture. Doing a little homework before you travel can provide an extra measure of security.

BE PRUDENT, NOT PARANOID

There are preemptive steps you can take to lessen the chance of danger. An excellent starting place is State Department website at www.travel.state.gov, which offers a wealth of general information regarding international travel, all indexed by topic for easy access. For information relevant to potential dangers, be sure to check the Consular Information Sheets look for Public Announcements, Travel Warnings and Travel Alerts.

Consular Information Sheets

Click on Country Specific Information on the website's home page to access Consular Information Sheets for every country in the world. These pages include information about the location of the U.S. Embassy or Consulate in the country, unusual immigration practices, health conditions, minor political disturbances, unusual currency and entry regulations, crime and security information, and drug penalties. If an unstable condition exists in a country that is not severe enough to warrant a Travel Warning, a description of the condition(s) may be included under an optional section titled "Safety/Security." Occasionally, the sheet may also restate any U.S. Embassy advice given to official employees. Generally, however, these pages simply present information in a factual manner so the traveler can make his or her own decisions.

Public Announcements

Public Announcements are accessed from the Consular Information Sheets. Once you have accessed the page for your country of interest, simply click Recent Embassy Notices for American Citizens. These notices are a quick way to obtain information about terrorist threats and other relatively short-term and/or transnational conditions posing significant safety risks. In the past, public announcements have been issued to deal with short-term coups, bomb threats to airlines, terrorist activity, and anniversary dates of previous terrorist events.

Travel Warnings and Alerts

Both Warning and Alerts are accessed from the website's home page. Travel Warnings are issued to describe long-term, protracted conditions such as the Iraq War or internal political turmoil that make a country dangerous or unstable. A Travel Warning is also issued when the U.S. Government's ability to assist American citizens is reduced due to closure of an embassy or consulate or downsizing of staff. Travel Alerts are issued to disseminate information about short-term conditions, generally within a particular country, that pose imminent risks to of U.S. citizens. Natural disasters, terrorist attacks, coups, anniversaries of terrorist events, election-related demonstrations or violence, and high-profile events such as the 2008 Beijing Olympics, are examples of conditions that might generate a Travel Alert.

Continued Vigilance

It is also a good idea to routinely check conditions even after you have arrived. Situations may change during your stay. Most newsstands have English-language newspapers. Also remember that every city has a few less-safe neighborhoods. If you're venturing out on your own to explore the city, talk to your host or hotel clerk so you know what areas, if any, to avoid.

STAY UNDER THE RADAR

In all our travels we have never felt alarmed or even threatened. However, caution is key. Avoid places where trouble is most likely to happen and keep a low profile. Here are few more things we've learned about staying safe.

Avoid Impressions of Wealth

Perhaps that advice sounds paradoxical in a book about traveling cheap. Remember that wealth is a relative term. Most middle-class American families have cell phones, digital cameras, and iPods. Dress the kids in trendy outfits from Target or K-Mart and, in some areas, you may easily give the appearance of wealth. Don't be overly loud, and always be polite. (If there is a problem, it's unlikely that anyone is intentionally trying to make things difficult for you. Be patient.) As mentioned in the previous chapter, you want to blend into the crowd.

Traveling on a cheap budget is often the best way to protect yourself from theft. Leave big rings and expensive watches or jewelry home. Take cameras out only when you need them. Don't hang them around your neck all the time - you are only advertising yourself as a target.

Don't flash a lot of money when purchasing food or tickets. (Remember, most of your money should be in the waist belt, with only enough for daily incidentals readily available.)

Don't Become Complacent

Always keep money out of the reach of those who may wish to relieve you of it. Do not get on crowded subways and buses. These are prime spots for pick-pockets, who stand back and target a tourist. As everyone pushes and shoves into the subway car, you will never notice as they remove items from your pocket or backpack. Large cities like Paris, London, Rome and New York are all prime targets for this kind of theft. Take your time, be smart, and wait for a less crowded bus or subway.

TIP: *Make sure you always keep your money belt safely out of sight and keep backpacks in front of you. Rome is the only place we have been successfully pick-pocketed. We had been traveling in the countryside for several weeks and had become too comfortable, carrying our money in a less secure manner. I continued this practice in Rome and was relieved of my cash in a matter of a few seconds.*

Be Mindful of the Pictures You Take

In certain countries it's okay to photograph some people and places but absolutely forbidden to photograph others. A good rule of thumb is to avoid photographing military installations or equipment, or even soldiers. If a place is guarded, you should ask if photographs are allowed. Avoid photographing official-looking and government buildings (the president's mansion, airports, dams and power plants)— just about anything that could be construed to be a target of future attack. Buy postcards instead. Also refrain from photographing poor people or slum areas. And whenever you want to take a picture of a specific individual or group, always ask permission first. Some cultures, particularly in Asia, have beliefs that ascribe very negative consequences to being photographed.

Most of the time, the rules for photography are posted at borders and airports as you enter a country. When in doubt, ask before you click. Every now and then you will find rules posted around the specific places that are prohibited. In many countries there is very little to worry about, but if someone is offended because you didn't ask, simply be polite and friendly, apologizing sincerely but without excessive remorse.

TIP: *Make sure you know the local laws and customs of the countries you are traveling through. (Consular Information Sheets are good for this.) Remember, while in a foreign country you are subject to the laws of that country.*

DO YOUR HOMEWORK

How safe you are, how well you survive mishaps, and how eager you are to travel again often depend on how much pre-planning you put into a trip. The details of "paper and plastic" (cash, traveler's checks, credit cards, passports, etc.) are discussed in Chapter 7. When you make copies of your documents and credit cards, be sure to leave one set with someone you trust at home. Include copies of drivers' licenses and airline tickets, so you will have reference numbers if everything is lost.

Insurance. Before leaving home thoroughly go over your insurance coverage. Find out if your personal property insurance covers loss or theft abroad. More importantly, find out whether your health insurance covers you abroad. Medicare and Medicaid do not provide payment for medical care outside the U.S. Even if your health insurance will reimburse you for routine care or services abroad, most policies do not pay for medical evacuation from a remote area or from a country where medical facilities are inadequate. Consider purchasing one of the short-term health and emergency assistance policies designed for travelers. Make sure that the plan you purchase includes medical evacuation in the event of an accident or serious illness.

To review . . .

- Use the State Department website to help plan your trip and stay apprised of potential safety risks.
- Avoid attracting attention.
- Be aware that pickpockets are everywhere. Keep belongings close and safe.
- Respect local rules and customs regarding photography.
- Prepare well so you don't encounter unpleasant surprises if something does go wrong
- Use common sense. Blend in, stay calm, and always know what is going on around you.

CHAPTER TEN

TO INFINITY
AND BEYOND

TO INFINITY AND BEYOND

B uzz Lightyear's response to any challenge is always "To infinity and beyond!" Full of big plans and big dreams, he believes anything is possible. In creating this book we hope to have shown you that extensive travel is also possible for everyday, ordinary families.

Have Kids–Will Travel was written first and foremost as a reference book on cheap/free travel, a book that will get you started on your family's next adventure. It is not a book that will bring you worldly wealth, but it can open the door to experiences that will give you a love of this planet greater than you have ever known. Because it creates personal connections to countries and cultures, travel provides an education far beyond what can be learned in books.

We have been blessed to have the opportunities to do the things we have done and see the things we have seen, but most importantly to learn the things we have learned and share them with our children. It is not easy planning trips like these with four children in tow, but the rewards always outweigh the cost (even when the trip isn't quite as free as we'd hoped).

As you get better and better at this low-cost travel, you will find times when you actually have more miles than you can possibly use. When this happens, we hope you will give those extra miles to help others. One way to do that is to donate them to Family Miracle Travel (FMT), a wonderful organization that offers free flights to folks in difficult circumstances. FMT has been set up to send families with special needs on what may possibly be their last vacation together. These are families where Mom, Dad, or maybe a child, has cancer or some other terminal disease and the burden of care-related expenses prohibits them from creating any more "big trip" memories.

If you know someone who can benefit from this service, or you wish to donate miles or contributions of time or money, please contact Family Miracle Travel at (435) 245-3208.

We also encourage service while traveling. Look for places where you and your children can give some meaningful service or even plan them into your adventure. Maybe an orphanage or a home for the elderly, wherever you go look for ways to make your trip a little more rewarding by serving those you come in contact with. This will bring you closer to the people and culture and help your children appreciate more the opportunities they have and be hopefully, a bit more grateful for what they have. If you have a desire to go to Peru, first read the book, *The Sunflower* by *New York Times* bestselling author, Richard Paul Evans, then you can visit and help at the actual orphanage he talks about in the book. Go to www.richardpaulevans.com/sunflower for more information.

Proceeds from the sale of *Have Kids–Will Travel* benefit Family Miracle Travel and other wonderful organizations including the Pulmonary Hypertension Association. Pulmonary hypertension is a rare blood vessel disorder in which the pressure in the pulmonary artery, the blood vessel connecting heart and lungs, rises above normal levels, often creating a life-threatening situation.

We hope you will enjoy your travel experiences as much as we are enjoying ours.

—The Bartlett Family

WORKSHEETS

HAVE KIDS—
WILL TRAVEL

Free Flights

Destination _____

Airline _____

# of People traveling _____

# of Points needed _____

Departure date _____

Length of stay _____

COLLECTING POINTS

Credit Card _____

Number of points per $1 spent _____

List of other partners (car rental, phone companies, internet provider etc)

_____

Number of points per $1 spent _____

_____

Number of points per $1 spent _____

_____

Number of points per $1 spent _____

free flights

Destination _____

Airline _____

# of People traveling _____

# of Points needed _____

Departure date _____

Length of stay _____

COLLECTING POINTS

Credit Card _____

Number of points per $1 spent _____

List of other partners (car rental, phone companies, internet provider etc)

_____

Number of points per $1 spent _____

_____

Number of points per $1 spent _____

_____

Number of points per $1 spent _____

Free Flights

Destination _____

Airline _____

# of People traveling _____

# of Points needed _____

Departure date _____

Length of stay _____

COLLECTING POINTS

Credit Card _____

Number of points per $1 spent _____

List of other partners (car rental, phone companies, internet provider etc)

_____

Number of points per $1 spent _____

_____

Number of points per $1 spent _____

_____

Number of points per $1 spent _____

Accommodations

Destination _____

# of Locations needed _____

    City Name _____

    City Name _____

    City Name _____

    City Name _____

    City Name _____

Home Exchange _____

Rental _____

Hotel Point Card _____

# of nights in home exchange _____

# of nights free hotel _____

# of nights for rental _____

# of nights paid hotel _____

Accommodations

Destination _____

# of Locations needed _____

City Name _____

City Name _____

City Name _____

City Name _____

City Name _____

Home Exchange _____

Rental _____

Hotel Point Card _____

# of nights in home exchange _____

# of nights free hotel _____

# of nights for rental _____

# of nights paid hotel _____

Accommodations

Destination _____

# of Locations needed _____

   City Name _____

   City Name _____

   City Name _____

   City Name _____

   City Name _____

Home Exchange _____

Rental _____

Hotel Point Card _____

# of nights in home exchange _____

# of nights free hotel _____

# of nights for rental _____

# of nights paid hotel _____

Transportation

••

Destination_____

# of days needed _____

TYPE OF TRANSPORTATION

Rental Car Company _____

    # of days _____

    Cost _____

Purchase Re-Purchase_____

    # of days _____

    Cost _____

Included in exchange _____

    # of days _____

Train ticket _____

    # of days _____

    Cost _____

Airline _____

    # of flights _____

    Cost _____

Transportation

··

Destination _____

# of days needed _____

TYPE OF TRANSPORTATION

Rental Car Company _____

    # of days _____

    Cost _____

Purchase Re-Purchase_____

    # of days _____

    Cost _____

Included in exchange _____

    # of days _____

Train ticket _____

    # of days _____

    Cost _____

Airline _____

    # of flights _____

    Cost _____

Transportation
....

Destination_____

# of days needed _____

TYPE OF TRANSPORTATION

Rental Car Company _____

    # of days _____

    Cost _____

Purchase Re-Purchase_____

    # of days _____

    Cost _____

Included in exchange _____

    # of days _____

Train ticket _____

    # of days _____

    Cost _____

Airline _____

    # of flights _____

    Cost _____

Budget

....

Destination_____

EXPENDITURES	QTY	BUDGETED	ACTUAL
Airline	_____	$_____	$_____
Transportation	_____	$_____	$_____
Accommodations	_____	$_____	$_____
Food	_____	$_____	$_____
Gasoline	_____	$_____	$_____
Attractions	_____	$_____	$_____
Treats	_____	$_____	$_____
Souvenirs	_____	$_____	$_____
Tolls/fee's	_____	$_____	$_____
Exchange rate fees	_____	$_____	$_____
Misc.	_____	$_____	$_____
TOTAL	_____	$_____	$_____

Budget

· ·

Destination_____

EXPENDITURES	QTY	BUDGETED	ACTUAL
Airline	_____	$_____	$_____
Transportation	_____	$_____	$_____
Accommodations	_____	$_____	$_____
Food	_____	$_____	$_____
Gasoline	_____	$_____	$_____
Attractions	_____	$_____	$_____
Treats	_____	$_____	$_____
Souvenirs	_____	$_____	$_____
Tolls/fee's	_____	$_____	$_____
Exchange rate fees	_____	$_____	$_____
Misc.	_____	$_____	$_____
TOTAL	_____	$_____	$_____

Budget

Destination_____

EXPENDITURES	QTY	BUDGETED	ACTUAL
Airline	_____	$_____	$_____
Transportation	_____	$_____	$_____
Accommodations	_____	$_____	$_____
Food	_____	$_____	$_____
Gasoline	_____	$_____	$_____
Attractions	_____	$_____	$_____
Treats	_____	$_____	$_____
Souvenirs	_____	$_____	$_____
Tolls/fee's	_____	$_____	$_____
Exchange rate fees	_____	$_____	$_____
Misc.	_____	$_____	$_____
TOTAL	_____	$_____	$_____